D0974628

To Pray God's Will

To Pray God's Will

Continuing the Journey

Ben Campbell Johnson

The Westminster Press
Philadelphia

Scripture quotations from the Revised Standard Version of the Bible are copyrighted 1946, 1952, © 1971, 1973 by the Division of Christian Education of the National Council of the Churches of Christ in the U.S.A. and are used by permission.

Some scripture quotations in this book are the author's own paraphrases.

Material in Chapter 6 from Alan Paton, *Ah, But Your Land Is Beautiful*, pp. 65–67, is copyright © 1981 Alan Paton. Reprinted with the permission of Charles Scribner's Sons.

Book design by Gene Harris

First edition

Published by The Westminster Press®
Philadelphia, Pennsylvania

PRINTED IN THE UNITED STATES OF AMERICA

9 8 7 6 5 4 3 2 1

Library of Congress Cataloging-in-Publication Data

Johnson, Ben Campbell.
  To pray God's will.

  1. Prayer. 2. Spiritual life—Presbyterian authors.
I. Title.
BV210.2.J62 1987   248.3   87-14272
ISBN 0-664-24085-2 (pbk.)

Contents

To Pray God's Will

Preface

The spiritual journey begins in mystery, and its pathway leads inevitably into the deeper mystery both of God and of ourselves. Who can explain how an ordinary person can be the focus of loving concern by a powerful Creator? Why would the Creator God choose to engage in fellowship with a weak and finite human?

God goes even further by inviting us to use our faculties and resources to search out the depths of this relationship. In Christ God bids us to pray, "Thy will be done." But how can we pray God's will? How can we approach the mystery of God? Certainly we cannot force the Almighty! Scripture says, "Do not say in your heart, 'Who will ascend into heaven?' (that is, to bring Christ down) or 'Who will descend into the abyss?' (that is, to bring Christ up from the dead)" (Rom. 10:6–7). Yet, if we have a sharp perception, the Lord God continuously approaches us, speaks to us, invites us into the Mystery.

To Pray God's Will offers the serious disciple six pathways into the Mystery. This book is not intended to be a road map that guides one directly to a chosen destination. Rather, these approaches are presented as the witness of one who has been led into the Mystery and offers a partial report of the journey. The Mystery has a peculiar interest in us; and if we listen, the Mystery will call us, entice us, and engage us. No two journeys will be alike, yet they will have enough similarity for one to be instructive of the other.

These half-dozen approaches to the Mystery have been one experience of being awakened by Love, being drawn into the darkness of faith, and "feeling" the Mystery as it impinges on every moment of human existence. Perhaps a description of the way will entice you to continue your journey.

You may wonder what this journey into Mystery holds. I will begin by suggesting a way of getting to know God better, a way of reflecting on the scriptures so that they are incorporated into your being. Another step on the journey will invite you to be open to your unconscious depths, to listen to those hidden parts of yourself that seek expression.

In addition to this inward journey, I will share with you a process for listening to God in the daily events of your life, a practice that integrates the content of each day into your faith story.

Then we will explore the spiritual desert, a symbol of aloneness, of solitude, where God matters supremely. This excursion will take us beyond rational thought or verbal description.

Because of the precarious nature of the journey, each of us needs companionship, a spiritual guide with whom we can share our discoveries and to whom we can turn for support and counsel. To assist you in finding such a friend, I will share with you my experience of recognizing the need, of seeking and finding someone to walk with me into the Mystery.

My report concludes with a perception of life from "the center." The inner journey leads to the center and to the kingdom vision, a vision of the new society, the new world. The knowledge of self and of God leads beyond the self to a transformation of the culture.

Perhaps a brief description of the adventure of *To Will God's Will: Beginning the Journey* would be instructive here. In that book I suggested that the journey metaphor aptly describes the spiritual life with its mixture of movement and rest. All of us are in the process of becoming what we have been destined for, some more nearly approximating it than others.

The beginning place for spiritual development lies within God's action in the formative events of our personal history. Each of us has a story woven around these turning points in our lives; by becoming aware of our story, we take note of the meaning it carries.

But our stories are more than human narrations about the events of our lives. They have been touched by a power outside ourselves, a transcendent power—God. Each story has a spiritual dimension, a divine aspect that houses the memory of the God who has touched us. God's encounter with us offers us the substance from which our spirituality develops.

After an exploration of how our story emerges from our history, I shared with you a way of shaping your life through prayer. I also suggested that the liturgy of worship is a form of corporate prayer.

The first portion of the journey concluded with a description of the focused life that finds expression in the prayer, "Thy will be done." The journey can be made with less confusion and distraction when our lives are unequivocally focused on God.

If you are joining the journey at this point, I suggest that you read the guidelines on journaling in Appendix B. Keeping a journal is an important aspect of this personal excursion in faith. Write in your journal the exercises for each chapter suggested in Appendix A. The spiritual journey must not be confined to an awareness of the principles and practices of spiritual growth; the journey must *be experienced to be understood*.

I offer myself to you as a guide, not because I think I am far enough ahead to advise you, but because so many persons are seriously seeking a deeper expression of faith and have no one to help them in their quest. Even in the churches many serious journeyers do not find direction, and many are groping in darkness without the companionship of others who are also making the journey into Mystery.

In these pages I have shared my life with you because I have been helped most by those who have told me their experiences of God. I believe that God has touched me; and if my recounting some of the ways this has occurred can be helpful to you, I will be grateful.

I cannot conclude these introductory remarks without another disclaimer. The experiences and insights I have been bold enough to relate have not made me perfect, or holy, perhaps not even very good. I do not belong to an elite group called "saints." About all I can say with integrity is that I have a deep interest in God. I want to know God. I want to learn in my own experience what it means to love God with all my heart. Thus, like you, I am a pilgrim on a journey, a journey to God, and I would delight in your company.

New Year's, 1987

1

Meditation
on the Journey

**The sacred journey leads to the center
of the primeval forest where the Mystery is
revealed.**

Once upon a time in the Far North there lived a young
man with the heart of an explorer. For as long as he
could recall he had pondered the question of being.
Intrigued by the things he could see and touch as well
as the fact of his inner being, he wondered, "Why is
there 'something' and not 'nothing'?" Day and night the
question plagued him until he could find no rest.

Then one day the matriarch of the village told him
that the answer to his question lay at the heart of the
primeval forest. In the center of the forest was a pool,
and the waters of the pool held the answer to the Mystery of Being. So the brave seeker set out to find the
forest and discover the pool.

After years of searching he found the enchanted forest, but there were no pathways into its heart. So another decade passed before, at last, he found his way
to the center of the vast wood. One day to his surprise
he happened upon a clearing in the depth of the forest.
At the center of the clearing lay a large, bubbling pool,
and beside the pool sat a bearded old man.

Filled with questions, the brave explorer approached
the old man eagerly, but before he could speak, the
ancient one silently motioned him into the pool and
then joined him. There he gently took the young man in

his arms and thrust him under the water. Coming up out of the water his eyes were opened; now he knew the reason for his being; now he knew why there was "something" and not "nothing."

The encounter with the Mystery of Being changed his heart, and the explorer wished to help his friends journey to the forest, discover the pool, and be immersed in its transforming waters. For a time the explorer clearly marked the pathways from the edges into the center of the primeval forest so others could find their way to the Mystery.

With his work completed it was, at last, time to return home and share with his village the wonderful news of his discovery. One after another said, "Tell us the meaning of being. Share with us the Mystery!"

But the explorer repeatedly urged, "Go and find out for yourselves!"

Knowing he could never tell the Mystery, he made a map of the primeval forest indicating the various pathways he had marked into the center.

The villagers pounced on the map, framing it and hanging it prominently in the town hall. All demanded for themselves a personal copy of the map. They even boasted to the neighboring village about their new possession.

But none of the folk in the explorer's village ever made the journey to the primeval forest; not one ever plunged into the pool; so none of them ever found the meaning of the Mystery.

It was enough for them to know that someone had made the journey. They felt secure just owning a map.

Perhaps the brave explorer did not know that at his birth the Mystery had left a mark in his heart sufficient to force the question and inspire the courage for the journey. His search for a pathway into the Mystery was a response to a gift that was given to him, even as ours is.

Where is the primeval forest that conceals the Mystery? How do we make our way through the thick woods and undergrowth to the center? The safest pathways to take have been identified, marked, and tested by thousands of previous pilgrims. The ways into the Mystery have alternately been described as meditation, contemplation, awareness, solitude, companionship, and vision. Each of these pathways, though different, leads to the center, to an encounter with the Mystery.

To travel these pathways requires the use of different faculties of the soul. In *A History of Christian Spirituality* Urban Holmes provides a succinct picture of these faculties that enable us to make the spiritual journey. His model has inspired the diagram below, which indicates four primary approaches to "the center."[1]

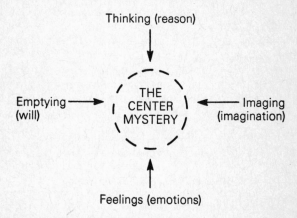

Like a compass face, the diagram indicates four primary approaches to prayer. Prayer may take a rational pathway to God, a way that uses reason to engage the mind. Bible study that seeks to understand the meaning of scripture qualifies as rational prayer. The speculative form of prayer gathers data, reflects on them, and applies the insights to life.

The "imaging" approach engages the imagination, paying special attention to spontaneous images that come to us in prayer. Using this faculty of the mind for Bible study enables us to project ourselves into the biblical text. This form of prayer substitutes images for words, participation for speculation.

Affective prayer approaches God through the emotions. This does not imply an emotionalism but a deepened awareness of our feelings. Affective prayer takes account of a range of emotions from "noticing with interest" to "love."

In *The Cloud of Unknowing,* one of the classic books on Christian mystical experience, the writer, an anonymous fourteenth-century Englishman, states that "God cannot be grasped by reason; God can be known through love." Jesus' greatest lesson on prayer may have been, "You shall love the Lord your God with all your heart." Feelings of concern about God and the desire for God are prayers of the heart.

The emptying form of prayer employs neither images nor feelings. *The Cloud of Unknowing* urges us to put all natural things below the cloud of forgetting and to face into the cloud of unknowing with neither images nor reason nor feelings. To pray in this fashion, the writer urges:

> Center all your attention and desire on him and let this be the sole concern of your mind and heart. Do all in your power to forget everything else, keeping your thoughts and desires free from involvement with any of God's creatures or their affairs whether in general or in particular. Perhaps this will seem like an irresponsible attitude, but I tell you, let them all be; pay no attention to them.[2]

As we explore the pathways of meditation, contemplation, awareness, solitude, companionship, and vision, each of these faculties will permit us to be opened more deeply to the Mystery. They should not be looked on as tools or as powers inherent in the self that give us the ability to find the Mystery ourselves. These are faculties of the soul, marks of the Creator through which the Divine Mystery manifests itself to human consciousness. The forms of prayer will draw first on one faculty, then on another; other forms of prayer will combine them in different ways to influence and shape the soul.

Meditation, a Way of Knowing God

Defining prayer as "loving God with your whole heart, soul, mind, and strength" implies the necessity of knowing God. Thomas Green says that persons cannot love what they do not know because real love demands knowledge.[3] Therefore, to love God with our whole being, we must get to know God. Meditation is one approach to the knowledge of God.

The Christian approach to meditation, in contrast to Eastern meditation, makes Christ normative for all knowledge. Christian meditation has often been confused with contemplation. Even a careful reading of spiritual writers results in confusion over the words "meditation" and "contemplation" because the writers use the terms in different ways. I use meditation to refer to active speculation about biblical texts, Christian symbols, and life experience. Contemplation for me refers to a receptive mode of the mind that draws on spontaneous imagination, affections, and the naked intent toward God in imageless prayer. The former uses reason, logic, and words; the latter depends on imagination, spontaneity, and intuition.

To meditate means to reflect on, to muse over. Christian meditation is the disciplined act of reflecting on the meaning of a word, an idea, or an experience. For example, we may meditate on the idea that "God is love." Reflecting on the love of God involves asking questions of it, turning it over in our minds, letting it draw forth other ideas that connect with it, and seeing this truth in a new light.

Meditation, as a disciplined act of focusing on a

Christian truth, symbol, or experience, has four movements: *awareness, attention, questioning,* and *application.*

Meditation begins with awareness. An idea strikes your consciousness; it seems to have meaning for you. Suppose you are reading the Gospel of John and encounter the verse, "I am the vine, you are the branches" (John 15:5). Something about this verse catches your attention. You have read it before, but this time you "notice" it in a different way. You become aware that it has a personal meaning that had somehow escaped you before.

The second movement in meditation is attention. Attention is your response to awareness; you give yourself to the idea that presents itself to you. You might say, "Christ is the vine, the source of my life. Can I imagine that relationship?" Attention has the quality of being present to an idea.

The third movement asks questions. Meditation systematically questions the idea and the images it inspires. For the verse cited above, the questions might be: What is the context of this verse? What did it mean to the first reader? How does it speak to me? What will I do? How will I change?

This analogy of the vine and branches comes from Jesus' last discourse to his followers. Possibly, the author was reminding the early church of its dependence on Christ. This text suggests to me the intimacy of Christ with his followers—the life in God sustains us all. Meditating on the answers to the questions that arise engenders other speculative questions; when we muse over these questions, the truth has an opportunity to grasp us firmly.

The fourth movement in meditation applies the insights to our lives. If the meaning I perceive from the "vine and branches" text points to the presence of the divine Spirit in my life—that is, the same life that flowed in Christ flows in me—will I trust myself to that life?

What would it mean for me to let this truth become a part of my life? What does this truth imply for the church?

This final movement often occurs just as I have described it—asking questions and making application to life. Yet there are times when the application seems to make itself and will strike our consciousness with such force that it requires no reflection, no application. For instance, the implication of our unity with God as suggested in "the vine and the branches" grasps us in a way that it makes its own application.

Meditational Knowing

On the spiritual journey there are two kinds of truth that we possess: "knowledge about" and "knowledge of." We have knowledge about the love of God, for example. Yet understanding all the words and repeating the words to others does not mean that we have trusted our lives to God's love. Knowledge of, on the other hand, means knowing in our own experience the ideas about which we speak; through our knowing we participate in God.

Consider a married couple. They have developed a workable relationship, yet one day the wife confesses to her counselor, "I have been married to Jim for seven years. We get along, have acceptable sexual relations, parent our sons, but I really don't know him." This couple knows each other in a surface way. They know external data *about* each other, but they lack knowledge *of* each other. To know each other—that is, to have *knowledge of* each other—requires time; it demands risk in sharing themselves. The intimacy for which this wife hungers will not be realized until both partners take the risk.

Likewise, we may know about God through the culture, through worship at church, through a catechism class, but this knowledge about God does not create intimacy with God. Intimacy requires risk, a risk often accompanied by fear. Do we fear what God might say if we listened? A friend of mine tells how his five-year-old son cried out in the night, "Daddy, I'm afraid. Come stay in the room with me." The father, attentive to the son's fear, went to his room and reassured him, "Son, you don't have to be afraid. God is here with you." Quickly the son blurted out, "Well, if he is, I sure hope he won't say anything!"

If we are afraid to get close to God, afraid to share our deepest self with God, afraid that God may speak to us, we will find numerous excuses to avoid a disciplined approach to meditation. Our fears will shield us from a consciousness of God's presence.

The experiential knowledge of God that we seek in meditation may be received in five ways: *recalling old truths,* the *illumination of the Spirit,* the *union of ideas previously isolated,* the *reception of new ideas,* and the *daring act of obedience to God.*

First, look at the recall of old but central truths stored in memory. Recall as a way of knowing is illustrated in Joshua's command: "This book of the law shall not depart out of your mouth, but you shall meditate on it day and night, that you may be careful to do according to all that is written in it" (Josh. 1:8).

The book of the law was known by the people of Israel; it had been given in a specific epoch in their history. Joshua exhorts them to reflect on what they already know so they can be faithful to its truth. As they meditate on truth long held, they will see new applications of it. An experiential knowledge of God often involves bringing to consciousness truths such as this that we have stored in our memory.

Experiential knowledge also occurs when the Spirit of God breathes on some truth that we have known for years—old truth becomes a new truth under the inspiration of the Spirit. There are truths we know about without having knowledge of them.

For example, I had been a minister for ten years. I had preached on the theme of God's love numerous times, saying with passion, "God loves you. Christ died for you." I recall the day, however, when the love of God became personal to me. I had been preparing a sermon on the love of God. As I was reflecting on the text, "something" whispered to me, "If you believe that I love all those persons to whom you will be speaking tomorrow, why can you not believe that I love you?" I listened to the question. I consciously made the choice to believe that God loved me! When these known words were breathed on by the Spirit of God, they changed me.

The knowledge of God comes from the union of two truths previously separated. For example, we may believe that God wills to be known to us. We may also believe that God can be known through the events of history. We point to the deliverance from Egypt, the cross of Christ, or the gift of the Holy Spirit at Pentecost as evidences of God's revelation within history. The twin facts that God (1) wills to be known and (2) designates human history as the arena of that revelation combine to enable us to see that God can be seen in the history of our lives, in the events that compose our narrative. Two insights unite to give greater significance to our personal journey. The compartmentalization of truth keeps us from having a holistic vision, and meditation is one way to get truth integrated.

The knowledge of God also comes through the encounter with new ideas. The sea of knowledge can never be fathomed. The infinity of truth around us contains the reality of God, which we shall never fully know. Yet each new insight that bursts on our consciousness mediates a fragment of the knowledge of God.

Jesus embodied a strange new idea that turned the intellectual house of Israel upside down. So disturbing to the elite was the idea that God would dare come among them in the flesh that they crucified him. They could not accommodate this radical idea of a God who took human form. Perhaps we should take care not to dismiss new ideas out of hand.

The knowledge of God sometimes comes through a daring act of obedience. Doing precedes knowing. In this instance the heart has reasons that the mind cannot comprehend. For example, we believe that God guides our lives, frequently giving this guidance through circumstances, such as the open door of opportunity. But when this confidence must be tested through a concrete choice, we may have to act without positive proof of God's direction.

Our will receives courage from a positive picture of the consequence of our choices. Imagination builds a bridge into the future. Yet our step of obedience is made in faith, and the knowledge of God's will is found in the action.

In human interaction, self-revelation affects both the revealer and the one to whom the revelation is made. I cannot reveal myself to you without having changes occur in both of us. The knowledge of God always produces change in us. In personal disclosure the one who reveals is also affected. I wonder what it means to God to become known to us.

Sources of Our Knowledge of God

How do we come to a knowledge of God? Toward what sources do we turn to receive God's revelation of the meaning of our personal journey? The standard sources of the journey are the *sacred scriptures* of the Old and New Testament, the *tradition* of the church, our *personal history*, and our *creative imagination*.

Anyone beginning to take the spiritual journey with greater seriousness must become firmly established in the foundational source of the knowledge of God—the Holy Bible. In this collection of books, composed over several centuries, God speaks. I do not view the Bible as a series of words dictated by God to a human secretary. Rather, the Bible is a record of events in which a people perceived God to be speaking. The story begins with Abraham, who heard God's call to leave his country and to establish a nation. God promised to give him a land; Abraham, believing God, obeyed and told this story to his children, and they to theirs. The narrative of God's dealing with the children of Abraham forms the backbone of the Old Testament. Of course, this story includes their laws, the rebuke and promises of the prophets, the wisdom of the proverbs, and the poetry of the psalms.

As we meditate on the writings of the Old Testament saints, we hear the same promises and admonitions of God to us today. Their experience of God is normative for ours.

The New Testament continues the story of God's people. The children of Abraham refused to recognize Jesus as the Messiah, so God's gracious action uniting all persons in Christ is yet to be fully recognized by the Jews. In the interim, the New Israel, the church, continues to fulfill the purpose of God.

When the early followers of Jesus told the story of his life, they connected it with the story of Abraham. For them it was one continuous piece of history. Their narrative contains his teachings and his deeds. The record we have suggests that they always told this narrative with the intent of proclaiming the transforming power of Christ's Spirit.

Paul, a later follower of Christ, reflected on the life and teachings of Jesus, giving a special place to his death and resurrection, and he interpreted the meaning of Christ for the Gentile world; that is, those who are not the children of Abraham. More than anyone else, Paul dealt with the question of the universal significance of Jesus Christ.

This story of the people who have listened to God and recorded God's word provides a source for our listening. As we reflect on the words of scripture, we

hear the Word of God spoken to us in our present situation. In our encounter with God through scripture, we
do not learn new scientific truth, or primarily historical
truth, but the truth about God's relation to us. To ask
more presses us beyond what the scriptures offer.
Urban Holmes observed that the Bible is poetry and
needs to be read as poetry; it evokes the right questions, hints at the answers, and leaves us sustained to
walk into the Mystery.[4]

Church tradition provides yet another source of our
knowledge of God. By tradition I mean the collection of
experiences, writings, and reflections of the followers
of Christ. Martyrs, church fathers, mystics, visionaries,
and saints are all our instructors. All of these in different
ways offer their insights into the nature and purpose of
God for the world. A few representative selections will
provide substance for your meditation:

Recall the often quoted affirmation of Augustine:
"Thou hast made us for thyself, O God, and our hearts
are restless until they rest in thee." Ponder the implications of that insight nestled in the long memory of the
church.

This prayer also offers another thoughtful meditation:

God be in my head and in my understanding.
God be in mine eyes and in my looking.
God be in my mouth and in my speaking.
God be in my heart and in my thinking.
God be at mine end and at my departing.[5]

Or permit this revision to speak to you:

God be in my head and in my understanding.
God be in my mind and in my thinking.
God be in my eyes and in my seeing.
God be in my mouth and in my speaking.
God be in my heart and in my loving.
God be in my hands and in my doing.
God be in my ways and in my walkings.
God be at my end and at my departing.[6]

Another gem has been called Saint Patrick's Breast-
plate.

> *Christ be with me, Christ within me!*
> *Christ behind me, Christ before me!*
> *Christ beside me, Christ to win me!*
> *Christ to comfort and restore me!*
> *Christ beneath me, Christ above me!*
> *Christ in quiet, Christ in danger!*
> *Christ in heart of all that love me!*
> *Christ in heart of friend and stranger!*[7]

Spend time with Saint Francis' prayer:

> *Make me, O Lord, an instrument of thy*
>   *peace.*
> *Where there is hatred, may I bring love;*
> *Where there is wrong, may I bring the spirit of*
>   *forgiveness;*
> *Where there is error, may I bring truth;*
> *Where there is despair, may I bring hope;*
> *Where there are shadows, may I bring light;*
> *Where there is sadness, may I bring joy.*
> *Grant, Lord, that I may seek to comfort rather than to*
>   *be comforted,*
> *To understand rather than to be understood,*
> *To love rather than to be loved,*
> *For it is by giving that one receives;*
> *It is by self-forgetting that one finds;*
> *It is by forgiving that one is forgiven;*
> *It is by dying that one awakens to eternal life.*[8]

At the turn of the century Charles de Foucauld wrote
the following prayer. It has spoken so powerfully to me
that I have committed it to memory and make it a fre-
quent prayer of my own.

> *Father, I abandon myself into your hands; do with me*
> *what you will. Whatever you may do, I thank you: I am*
> *ready for all, I accept all.*
> *Let only your will be done in me, and in all your crea-*
> *tures. I wish no more than this, O Lord.*

Into your hands I commend my soul; I offer it to you with all the love of my heart, for I love you, Lord, and so need to give myself, to surrender myself into your hands, without reserve, and with boundless confidence, for you are my Father. Amen.[9]

In addition to the scriptures and the treasury of the church, our own personal history provides us with a knowledge of God. Each life is an incarnate word of God, a lived expression of God's self. Humans have been made in the image of God and bear God's likeness, a metaphor confessed from the beginning. While aware of our likeness to God, we have been less perceptive of the revelation of God in our own sacred stories. These stories of our lives carry a deeper significance; they express not only the meaning of our lives but a unique word that God speaks.

If we are to hear that word, we must imaginatively review the events that have given substance to our life story. We must engage them again, listen to them with sharper attention, and discern in them what God is saying. As we make our life the subject of meditation, we reflect on it, raise questions, and make new connections just as we do when meditating on scripture. Augustine's *Confessions* is an example of this intensive reflection on life from the perspective of faith in Christ.

The providence of God lies hidden in the events of each life. Lest an encounter with the Divine Spirit wipe out our humanity, this providential work of God may operate quite imperceptibly at a given moment but becomes clearer when we listen back to the sounds of God in our life. God comes incognito in the guise of events that shape, direct, inspire. God illuminates our thoughts and awakens our imagination. Yet this intervention occurs so gently that we possess perfect freedom to be our self and choose our own path. How marvelous! How mysterious!

When I was forty years old, I had to make an important decision in my life. As part of the decision process,

I began to review the chapters of my life.[10] "To what have I given myself for the past twenty years of ministry?" I asked. "What are the things that I like to do? What do I do best?" I recalled my pastoral ministry, participation in a nationwide renewal movement, the reception of a doctoral degree. I felt an urge to use my creative ability, my love of writing, my ability to relate to people. A seminal influence in my thinking was the promise God had recently impressed on my mind: "The gifts and calling of God are irrevocable" (Rom. 11:29). My meditation led me to believe that God had called me to remain in my present ministry. Reflecting on the data of my life mixed with the inspiration of God provided the material for the decision.

Our knowledge of God comes from yet another source—our imagination. By imagination I do not mean that we create reality, that we dream up the knowledge of God as if it were a fairy tale. Imagination gives us the capacity to name the unknown, to create the new, and to leap out of the familiar into the unknown. Imagination is creative; it takes a bold leap forward in knowing before the knowledge has been fully formed. I think that imagination is the partner of intuition; it takes the unformed products of intuition and gives them a shape and a name.

Let me illustrate how imaginal knowing functions. For seven years I felt that my life had been set on a shelf. I had no question about the love of God, or about God's purpose for my life. For those years it seemed, however, that God had forgotten about me. In the sixth year a stirring of the Spirit began in my deep unconscious. My interest in knowing God and relating to God's purpose for my life intensified. I found my hunger for the Transcendent growing; prayer became important to me. I found myself listening more intently for God. During this time I made a three-day silent retreat, a first for me.[11] The retreat marked a watershed: subsequent to that retreat I had a conviction that God was indeed dealing with my life. Confident that God had a purpose for me, I struggled along waiting for the revelation of God's will. Out of that struggle I heard a word from God: "You are a servant of the Lord, in waiting." This idea that came to my mind was not an audible statement. In the silence the idea appeared in my consciousness. It spoke to me. It came "against" me as though it were not of my own production. During those months while I waited for the revelation of God's will, the awareness of the divine purpose coming from the depths of my being resisted a name; it had no form. How was I to be the servant of God? I experienced this consciousness as an energy compelling me toward God and assuring me that God had a purpose for me. But only when the call came to my present position could I give a definite name to this servanthood.

An Approach to Meditational Knowing

Since there is no single meditation technique that is best for everyone, a few introductory guidelines may prove helpful. In your first efforts at meditation find a setting that is conducive to quiet reflection. Certain rooms in the house seem more conducive than others. I like the den with a comfortable chair. You may prefer an outdoor setting.

Next, choose the material for your meditation—scripture, a gem from the treasury of the church, a chapter from your past life, a dream, or an issue for your future.

When you have selected the subject for your meditation, get seated comfortably. Relax. Read or think about the material. Don't work at meditation. Take a casual, receptive approach. If you have chosen a passage of scripture, for example, read it over. Think about it. Let the words leap from the page. Permit an idea to grasp you. How does it apply to your life? Mull over the ideas. Permit them to speak their message.

You will find the selections printed in this chapter good sources for meditation. Memorize these prayers.

As you memorize, ask questions of each phrase of the prayer. Listen to its message.

A meditation on the meaning of your life will also be helpful. You will receive guidance, a greater integration of your life, and intuitions about your future.

The discipline of meditation provides one way to open ourselves to Christ, who wills to live his life through us. Your interest in the subject indicates a hunger for the presence of Christ. As you give time to this intense reflection, a passion for the will of God will begin to possess you more completely. As God's Spirit grasps you, your life will show evidence of God's presence—obedience, service, a passion for justice and peace. The experience that affects us so deeply within expresses itself outwardly in our actions and vision.

You will find suggestions for meditation in the exercise for chapter 1 in Appendix A. And if you have not already done so, read the material on journaling in Appendix B and begin today to keep a spiritual journal.

2

Journey Into the Contemplation of God

Christ is the image of the journey into fellowship with God.

The spiritual journey passes through our personal history into an encounter with the origin of our being, the Creator God. To listen to our own depths requires a sensitivity to the language of the soul. We receive this sharpened awareness through another pathway into the Mystery—the contemplation of God. In our discussion of meditation we underscored the use of our rational faculty to analyze, reflect on, and discern truth. In contemplation the faculties of imagination and feeling take precedence over reason. In meditation the mind is active in the pursuit of the knowledge of God, while in contemplation it functions in a receptive mode, permitting the truth of God to come to it.

The Meaning of Contemplation

Probably no word in the vocabulary of spiritual writers is more ambiguous than "contemplation." Each writer defines contemplation from a slightly different perspective. Saint Teresa of Avila draws an analogy of the garden to explain this type of prayer. "Contemplation," says Saint Teresa, "is like a garden which receives its water in a variety of ways in order to produce flowers and fruit. The garden is our life; the way it is watered, our prayer." Prayer answers the question: "How do we get the water to the garden in order that the flowers may grow and bloom?" In four ways.

First, we may draw the water by hand. This method requires a great deal of effort like that required by structured prayer. In this form of prayer we adopt a plan; set a time to meet God each day; war against wandering thoughts; and persist in our efforts despite weariness and the temptation to neglect it.

A second way to bring water to the garden is through the use of a windlass to draw the water from its underground pool. The windlass is analogous to meditation in which we discipline our minds to ask questions of the scriptures, muse over the chapters of our lives, or reflect on issues that affect our future. This way of prayer requires somewhat less effort than the former.

Irrigation provides yet a third way of watering the garden. This form of prayer is comparable to meeting God in corporate worship. While corporate worship requires effort, it does not require as much energy as meditation. The congregation prays the liturgy even when some individuals fail to participate. The worshiping community carries us when our own strength fails.

Finally, the garden may receive water from the rain, over which we have no control. This form of watering is like contemplation in which we place ourselves in the presence of God and receive what God offers us. This communion comes as a gift, not as something earned through merit or effort. Contemplation opens us to the unconscious movement of the Spirit of God in the depths of our being.

In contemplation we do not aim to acquire new information, but to expose our consciousness to God by becoming present to the Presence. Quite often nothing seems to be happening. We feel empty and alone, afraid that we are wasting our time; but, unknown to us, the Spirit falls on the dry, parched ground of the soul.

In addition to Saint Teresa, other travelers on the

spiritual journey have also described contemplation.
Saint Thomas, the theologian; John Tauler, the mystic;
Ignatius, the disciplinarian; and Thomas Merton, the
saint. Saint Thomas defined meditation as "reason, a
discursive deduction from the principles of truth." Contemplation for him was the "simple, intuitive vision of
the truth." Compare his definition with Tauler's: "Verbal
prayer is but the clothing, not the person of prayer. In
the essence of prayer, the heart and mind go out to God
without an intermediary—the lifting of the mind to God
in love." Saint Ignatius makes a succinct distinction.
"Meditation is thinking about God; contemplation is
looking at scenes from the life of Christ." Thomas
Merton says, "A contemplative is one who makes use
of all the resources of theology and philosophy and
art and music in order to focus a simple, affective gaze
upon God."

These dependable guides help us see that contemplation demands a receptive frame of mind. Like the
garden receiving rain, the mind envisions truth, a vision
that comes not through our efforts but through God's
grace. We experience a union with God that fulfills
Paul's injunction to "let this mind be in you, which was
also in Christ Jesus" (Phil. 2:5, KJV). The chief source of
our contemplation is the life of Christ as we seek to see,
hear, and feel his presence in our lives. But our contemplation cannot be limited to the life of Christ or even the
scriptures. According to Merton's theology, philosophy, art, and music also provide abundant material for
the contemplation of God.

But why this emphasis on contemplation? The most
basic answer is the love of God, but there is another
dimension. Because an encounter with God produces a
corresponding encounter with one's self, contemplation opens the self to new depths, enabling us to find
new direction, integration, healing, and perhaps useful-
ness in God's kingdom. The journeyer, therefore, must
first consider the nature of the self that opens to the
vision of God.

The Nature of the Contemplative Self

What is the nature of the self seeking to encounter God in the silent sanctuary of the spirit? As I have already indicated, each of us is an individual self, a self in some ways separate from every other. Each is, therefore, a unique, unrepeatable, miracle of God. We are at the same time joined to every other person; we belong to the family of God and must recognize our dependence on others. In fact, only in relationship to other persons do we discover the fulfillment of ourselves. The contemplative journey must not become a perverted individualism isolating us from other persons. To the extent that our search for God becomes private, we miss the clearly revealed will of God to create a community of persons for his glory. The journey is personal but never private.

The encounter with God in human consciousness occurs from within and without. The "without" meeting occurs through the word of God that confronts us with a call, a challenge, or judgment. This encounter has a deeply personal character as God speaks with authority to redirect our lives. In this meeting God has the character of an absolute "I" who meets us as a "thou."

The meeting with God from within occurs with God's confrontation; it has a more subtle character and comes through the unconscious depths. God speaks, but not in words of direct address. The communication appears more gently in human consciousness, like bubbles floating to the surface of a pond. The communication comes in symbols that must be interpreted. The manner in which we listen to this subtle but elusive communication is called "contemplation." The discovery of this depth within requires us to take a look at the roles of memory, imagination, and the unconscious.

As self-conscious, reasoning selves we have a memory. We have the capacity to store experience and to call it up at a future time. Memories carry forward knowledge gained from experience. Dr. Wilder Penfield, the neurosurgeon turned researcher, has compared the human brain to a giant computer. That computerlike part of our anatomy stores all our experiences. In his experiments Dr. Penfield demonstrated that an electrical shock to a certain portion of the brain stimulated memories stored there. A shock to the portion adjacent to the first stimulated a subsequent memory. This evidence suggested to him that all our experiences are stored sequentially in our brain. With effort they can be brought to consciousness.[1]

Urban Holmes compares the memory to a cylinder. The cylinder is open at both ends and layered with memories like a parfait. On the topside of the cylinder the mind engages in daily experience, the data of awareness; at the lower end, the energy of God impinges on memory. Holmes, relying on the ideas of theoretical physicist David Bohm, suggests that this energy is the fundamental source of matter and consciousness. Holmes concludes, "Our memory has a bottom and that bottom is the mystery of divine creativity, waiting to be known." This power exists; it impinges on the deepest level of our consciousness, but its power comes on us in code. "Yet that bottom," says Holmes, "is what sustains us." We can know God only in God's essence as this power manifests itself in our consciousness; when it does, we give it names, names taken from our conscious experience. Holmes says that "the energy of God as it infuses the person is spontaneously clothed in an incarnate form."[2]

Think about the picture Penfield and Holmes paint of this deep memory. Our memory stores all our life experiences. At the most fundamental level the Ultimate Energy in the universe acts on our memory, stimulating symbols in our deep self, uniting itself to them, and entering our consciousness in an incarnate form. In contemplation we open ourself to this Divine Energy, inviting it to manifest itself in our consciousness with words, feelings, and images. In this act we meet not a faceless, impersonal power but the Creator God who loves us and unites with us.

In addition to being a remembering self, we are also an imagining self. We not only have the power of recall but the power to project ourselves into an imagined future. With our creative imagination we call the future into being, giving us quick passage out of the present into an imagined future.

We can imaginatively enter into another's experience. In reading a novel, for example, I identify so strongly with a character that for the moment I become that person. Through this identification I experience the feelings of the hero or the villain. Recall when you have been so engrossed in a movie that it "happened" to you. Your imagination gave you the power of participation. But do not confuse imagination with unreality. Imagination creates your reality; it places an image on the mass of unnamed experience that enables you to differentiate it from other experiences and thereby to reflect on it and weave it into the fabric of your self.

Beyond human consciousness, deeper than memory and creative imagination, each of us has an unconscious self, a self relatively unknown and autonomous. This deeper mind stores the commands that keep the body functioning. It causes the heart to beat, the temperature to be stabilized, and the glands to secrete. These functions are all out of the reach of the human intellect or volition.

The unconscious contains a ground plan for our lives, including the potentiality for bodily development and intellectual capability. That ground plan contains our basic orientation to life: the way we prefer to gather data, how we like to relate to others, our preference for a particular style of decision making.

In the unconscious we have received all our potential. These gifts, possibilities, and preferences are not under conscious control, but they impinge on our consciousness. In their own language they seek to reveal to us our life plan; these potentials within us get our attention with pain or anxiety; they speak to us in symbols and intuitions.

Contemplation engages the whole person, but it focuses on the deep unconscious stream of being beyond the reach of mind or will. To become receptive to the powers of the unconscious, especially the potentiality stored there, we can use contemplation to call on both memory and imagination. Memory researches the past with both its achievements and possibilities, while the imagination pictures what is possible in the future. Through the use of both memory and imagination, the conscious self integrates the past with the future and guides life toward wholeness and meaning.

Through the work of contemplation the actualization of our potential and the shaping of our future occur in the presence of God. The God who is our Creator, who impinges continually on our deep memory, seeks to communicate to us in symbols without destroying our humanity. To receive God's communication, we must learn God's speech and the doorways through which God enters.

Doorways Into the Deeper Self

Persons on the life journey live on different levels simultaneously. Consciousness receives messages from the external world of things and persons, but it also receives images and feelings from the subconscious dimension of memory and imagination. Probably the most forceful conditioners of our feelings and decisions arise from the unconscious. Because of the powerful influence the depths of life have on our life journey, we need to learn how to listen to our depths, even to intervene in halting some of the impulses that compel us.

In seeking to understand the nature of this deeper self, I have been enlightened by the thinking of Ira Progoff, a student and interpreter of Carl Jung. While not himself a confessed believer in Jesus Christ, Progoff has created a structure of thought that is compatible with Christian faith. He offers six major proposals.

First, there is a reality lying beneath all appearances that seeks to communicate itself. This reality, which we call God, is separate from the appearance of things but does not constitute a separate spiritual world. This reality communicates itself through the world of appearances.

Second, God communicates through symbols rather than through propositional statements. The primary example of God's symbolic communication is Jesus Christ. God did not send a telegram to the world; God sent the Son. Prior to sending the Son, God became known through the concrete symbol of the creation.

Third, the symbols through which the depth dimension communicates itself have three characteristics. A symbol points toward a mystery that cannot otherwise be known. All of nature symbolizes the Creator; it speaks of the mystery of the incomprehensible God. A symbol carries a meaning that transcends itself. For example, a nation's flag is more than its shape and color; it represents the history of a country and evokes patriotic feelings among the citizens. Finally, a symbol carries a meaning that grasps persons, but this meaning cannot be reduced to logic, analysis, or rational descriptive statements. We can endlessly analyze the cross according to the various theories of the atonement and still not adequately explain why that symbol evokes such powerful feelings in persons.

Fourth, this reality prefers to make itself known in an atmosphere of reverence. A reverent attitude toward the mystery of being opens us to it and enables us to participate in its unfolding through our personal consciousness. Receptivity requires sensitivity to, and respect for, the symbolic dimension of our being. The journey into the depth dimension passes through sacred ground that inspires within us an attitude of awe and reverence.

Fifth, this underlying reality gives being to everything that is, but this reality is not an object separated from us. We could not be if we did not participate in the power of being that this reality supplies. We can, however, make no claim on this reality, although this reality is always present to us.

Sixth, we can be drawn into this depth dimension, listen to it, and through our choices and actions actualize it in life. We Christians call this depth reality "God." Through our awareness of God's will and purpose and our choices to cooperate with God, we increase a consciousness of reality in the modern world. Explicitly, as we open ourselves to the presence of God that underlies all things, we incarnate a form of the presence in the world of our experience.[3]

How does God become known through our unconscious? How does the God of the depths become manifest in human consciousness? Like a tree exposed to the atmosphere, the human unconscious is always exposed to the presence of God. It is as though our depths had their grounding in God. The activity of God in the unconscious serves as a stimulus that manifests itself in consciousness as thoughts, feelings, and ideas. At the unconscious level, God comes as God wills and speaks as often or as seldom as God wills. When God's communication rises to our awareness, we may or may not recognize the Divine Presence.

We must not identify God with the unconscious. To do so would make us little deities. In this life we do not receive that one-to-one union with God. We must also note that the dark side of creation also has access to the unconscious. The demonic, destructive power of darkness and evil can also erupt through the unconscious. The dark side consists of our own repressed guilt and fear and transcendent evil.

In contemplation we aim to open ourselves to the depths of our soul, to face our dark side in the presence of Christ, and to integrate it into our conscious self. The more we integrate the unconscious content into our lives, the more the mask we wear melts away, and the more we fulfill the will of God.

The form of those messages from the deeper level of awareness will vary. One form of communication is found in our dreams. Dreams, according to Freud, symbolize the conflict between the life drive and our conscience. This primal conflict creates tension that we repress. Because of our inability to admit this conflict to consciousness, the deep mind finds release through dreams.

Carl Jung, like Freud, recognized the power of dreams to resolve tension, but he saw more. Jung held that dreams, in addition to resolving conflict, communicated the deeper mind. Through symbols common to the human race, the deeper self signals unrealized possibilities, unacknowledged longings, and even hints of the future. A few experiences with the deeper self will cause us to take this level of reality seriously and to listen more intently to the message of our dreams.

Our deeper memory also speaks to us through hunches and intuitions. An intuition does not result from logical, rational thought but comes apparently uncaused, breaking in on us "out of the blue." Such an experience came to me in January 1979. I wanted to structure the year by writing down my goals for the next twelve months. I began the process by asking, "What do I really want to do this year?" I closed my eyes, relaxed, and listened.

As I listened, a number of ideas came to my mind. Many of them focused on immediate goals, work to accomplish, persons to write, projects to finish. But two strange ideas surfaced. First, I had the idea to pastor a church. Indeed, I wondered where that idea came from because twenty years before when I left my former pastorate, I thanked God that part of my life was finished. Nevertheless, I wrote on my list for 1979 "pastor a church."

The other strange idea was "Finish your Ph.D. because one day you may wish to teach." So I added this to my list. Since both ideas remained clear and forceful in my mind, I began to pursue them.

In less than six months I had been chosen to conduct an interim pastorate. I was also readmitted to Emory University's Ph.D. program, which I had abandoned eight years earlier. Like many graduate students, I had finished all the requirements but the dissertation. I felt a unity within myself as I pursued both of these goals. Two years later, when I had finished the Ph.D., I had an encounter that explained the meaning of these two intuitions.

One Saturday my wife and I were sitting in a restaurant at a shopping mall near our home. Looking up, I saw a friend, Robert Ramey, the professor of ministry at Columbia Seminary. I dashed to the door and called to him. He came into the restaurant and sat down with Nan and me.

I began, "Bob, I want you to celebrate with us. I have finally finished the degree program I began seventeen years ago." Being a sensitive soul, Bob shared our joy. He and I had known each other for several years. As a local pastor, he had used a program I had developed through the Institute of Church Renewal, and he had written materials the organization had published. Two years before, he had accepted a call to become a professor at the seminary.

The conversation bounced from one subject to another until I said quite bluntly, "Bob, I'm planning to ask your president for a job."

"You are? What do you want to teach?" Bob asked.

"Evangelism. That's what I've done throughout all my ministry, and that's what I know best."

Bob's interest picked up. "Do you know about the grant?"

"What grant?" I inquired.

"Columbia Seminary has recently received a grant of one hundred and fifty thousand dollars to hire a professor of evangelism."

"What qualifications are you looking for?"

"We want a person who is coming from the pastorate, who has a Ph.D. degree, and who has skills in developing models and programs for evangelism."

I could hardly believe my ears. A pastor, a Ph.D., and a creator of models—a task I had been involved with for twenty years.

"With whom can I talk about the job?" I asked excitedly.

Without batting an eye, Bob said, "Well, Ben, I'm chairman of the search committee."

That was indeed a numinous encounter. God had spoken to me through my deeper self two years earlier, and the plan for my life was coming together in God's timing.

When we are united to Christ, our desires often reflect his will. Some of us have been taught that anything we desire must be evil because it comes from self and not from Christ. Who is to say that Christ cannot speak through the soul's sincere desire? The will of God written into our unconscious does speak, I believe, through the deep desires of our heart. Not all our desires are to be equated with the will of God, but desires attended by the mind and purified by the Word of God can reveal God's intention.

Buried deep within every human there is a dream, often secret, for what the dreamer most deeply desires. Fears, doubts, and feelings of inadequacy often hide this unacknowledged dream, but it refuses to go away because the creative Spirit of God has stamped it in the depths of our being. There it waits to be attended and acted on. On occasion we admit it momentarily to consciousness. It sits before us tentatively, like a butterfly on a rose, then slips away. The image of our longing appears too good to be true, and fearfully we turn away from what we most deeply desire. Can we not begin to believe that God wills good things for us?

A woman in her fifties entered seminary to complete

her dream career. Before her senior year we conducted her professional assessment. Hesitantly she discussed a number of possibilities for her future—administrator, chaplain, pastor, associate pastor.

I asked her, "Mary, what do you really want to do?" Immediately she confessed, "I would like to be an associate minister in charge of pastoral counseling."

"Why don't you risk it?"

The entire committee supported her decision. She began a year's internship to prepare for the one thing she most deeply desired. She really knew what she wanted but was afraid to believe that she could achieve it. This deeper self speaks to us through our most heartfelt desires. Where can we get the confidence and courage to listen to our deeper self?

On another occasion I asked a brilliant man of thirty-five, "What's your dream?" He quickly replied, "To get a Ph.D. and teach in a seminary."

"What holds you back?"

"I'm afraid I may not have what it takes."

I pressed him. "Does God place a dream like this in your heart to tease you? Would God seduce you with the image of grand service only to have you fail?"

Listen to your life dream. God often speaks through it.

The deeper self also speaks through "twilight imaging." I have borrowed this term from Ira Progoff, who teaches the technique in his intensive journal workshops. Twilight imaging denotes a state between focused consciousness and daydreaming. It is a state of "relaxed receptivity." To enter this state, relax your body physically; let your mind be open; give attention to the images that appear. As these images appear, let your imagination follow them, taking you wherever it will.

I had an experience of twilight imaging in prayer that has been very significant to me. I began by relaxing, closing my eyes, and looking at the images that appeared before me. I saw a golden field of wheat blowing in the wind. The field sloped down to a small, white, framed chapel nestled in a patch of woods. I made my way to the chapel, opened the door, and entered. No one was inside. At the front stood a pulpit with a Communion table before it. On the table were a loaf of bread and a cup of wine.

Behind the pulpit were two wall hangings. On one were the words *Holy, holy, holy, Lord God Almighty, heaven and earth are full of your glory, glory be to you, O Lord most high.* The other wall hanging carried a prayer of abandonment that began, *Father, I abandon my soul into your hands. Do with me what you will.* I sat down on the front pew to listen to what God had to say to me. God did not speak. I heard no words, yet I was aware of being in the Transforming Presence.

After sitting in the presence of the Spirit for a while, I noticed behind the pulpit a spiral staircase leading to an underground room. At the end of the stairs I discovered a brightly lighted room with a stream running through it. To the left the stream ran in darkness through a tunnel, but to the right it opened to a bright light that revealed a lush garden and a white-sand beach. In this underground cavern beneath the chapel, new rooms with fascinating furnishings appear each time I visit using twilight imaging.

When I visit this chapel with its deeply buried secrets, I am engaged quickly by the presence of God. The images come from a sacred spot in the depths of my being where visual images open to me a deeper awareness of myself. Each symbolizes a part of me. Together they are a symbolic representation of the content of my psyche. In the silence of these various rooms of my soul the Spirit grasps and shapes my being. Through these symbols the deeper self makes itself known; and the more fully known and integrated it becomes, the more whole do I become as a self.

All these various avenues—dreams, desires, visions

of the future, twilight imaging—have value on the spiritual journey, but contemplation of scripture is the soundest way of listening to the deeper self. Because the images and truth of scripture are normative for the Christian experience of God, contemplation draws on these symbols of the faith to inspire our imaging.

The contemplation of events in Jesus' life includes aspects of these other approaches to the deep self. This way also focuses on our deepest desires; it includes imaging ourself in the presence of Christ and being in dialogue with him; it also involves responding to our intuitions.

By contrast, however, this approach to prayer engages the imagination through scripture. We listen for the word of God through the words and events of Jesus' life as a personal revelation to us today. Likewise, listening to the words of Paul, for example, we read our lives into each particular situation. Through these words of scripture, God speaks to us in our contemporary situation.

Three Forms of Contemplative Prayer

The contemplation of scripture that I am recommending has three sequential parts: description, dialogue, and dedication.

The descriptive aspect of contemplation requires entering a passage as one of the participants. Think of yourself as a person in the story and retell the events in the first person. Here is an illustration using Mark 2:1–12.

I was in Capernaum busily at work when I heard that Jesus was home again. My heart filled with expectation, I ran down the street to his house. A crowd had already gathered, but I moved as near the door as I could. The crowd pressed upon me. Still others kept coming until there was no room at all.

He began to speak. He told us that God's rule was breaking in. I didn't know what that meant. While I was listening with rapt attention, suddenly I felt a push by a man carrying a stretcher. He and three others were carrying a paralyzed man. He wanted to get through, but neither I nor those around me moved. We got there first. Why should we give up our place?

Still trying to listen, I saw the four go behind the house. Suddenly, this paralytic was lowered in front of Jesus. I had tried to get close to Jesus myself, but now this fellow had been given the place of honor right at his feet.

Jesus glanced up at the four on the roof, turned to the paralytic, and said, "Your sins are forgiven." Just like that! He noticed this man. He spoke to an issue central in his life. I wondered if he knew I was there. I wondered if my own sins could be wiped out. How I have struggled with my doubts and fears. Could he resolve them? I wanted everything in me clean—nothing left to weigh me down.

Then he spoke to the scribes. They must have questioned Jesus' authority to absolve the man of sin.

He spoke again: "Which is easier? To forgive or heal—to settle the past or empower for the future?" Then he told the paralyzed man, "Get up and get on with your life!"

He did! The man got up, picked up the stretcher, and walked, then ran, toward his home in the village. The sight stirred my longing to be whole myself. . . . But how can I, sinful man that I am, find this wholeness?

This first-person narration permits you to participate in Jesus' encounter with the paralyzed man.

The second aspect of contemplation calls for an imaginative dialogue with Jesus. As if you were the person in the narrative with whom you have identified, begin the dialogue with Jesus by asking the most natural question in your consciousness. As a man in the

crowd, I talk with Jesus about the hunger for forgiveness and cleansing that has surfaced in my awareness
by Jesus' healing of the paralyzed man.

The man in the crowd engages Jesus in dialogue:

*"When I heard you had come back, I felt a sudden
hope that my deepest longing could be fulfilled. I came
to listen, only to be irritated by these four men deter-
mined to bring their friend to you. But when you spoke
to him, I felt my hope rise. Maybe I, too, could be
forgiven. As I watched him leave, I longed to be as
free and whole as he was. [Pause] Lord, can you make
me whole, too?"*

*"It is not whether I can make you whole, but can you
trust me? Can you give me your life? Will you let me
mold your will?"*

"I can. I will give my life to you. Your will be done!"

*"That's an easy prayer for you today. Will you say it
when life threatens you? Will you believe then that I am
in the events of your life doing my will?"*

*"I don't know. It is my desire to pray then as I pray
today, no matter what happens."*

*"I am not finished with you. I have a task for you to
do. It is very important for you to listen for me. Trust me
even when you do not see any evidence. Keep bringing
your paralysis to me. . . . Yes, you were also forgiven
when I spoke to the man. I felt power go out of me to
you. You are forgiven, accepted completely."*

Contemplative prayer should always conclude with
an offering of our life to Christ. The prayer of dedication
is our response to what Christ has spoken to us through
the meditation.

*"Lord, I have been an onlooker for so long. I have
seen you heal the lives of others, and I have longed for
the wholeness and freedom I have witnessed in them.
I offer you my life today with its paralysis. Make me
whole. I hear the word you speak to me about 'not being*

finished with me.' I offer my life to you in whatever way you choose to use me. Do with me whatever you will."

This illustration of imaginative prayer shows at once that the scripture draws forth the deeper self. The material in my imaginative description is not about the man in the crowd; it is about me. Do you see how the scripture serves as a magnet to elicit the deepest part of the self and draw it into the presence of God? The scripture in this way mediates the healing, redemptive presence of Christ at the point of our need. In this illustration the words and ideas came from the life of the writer, but they also communicated the presence of God. These revelations cannot be manufactured; they cannot be manipulated. Yet, we can put ourself in the place to hear God speak to us. We can listen contemplatively.

I am eager for you to encounter God through contemplation because this meeting unites you with God's intention for you. In this renewed awareness your soul finds the strength and energy to do the will of God. In the power of the Spirit you will make choices and the necessary sacrifices to make God's kingdom a reality on this earth.

The exercise for chapter 2 in Appendix A offers a number of scripture passages to use as an approach to contemplation. Write your responses in your journal.

3

Listening to God in the Present Moment

Wise journeyers listen to the word being spoken in their own sacred existence.

Listening to our unconscious brings to our awareness an assortment of insights into ourselves and God. Opening this part of ourselves with which we have had little acquaintance heals us, expands our awareness, and releases new energy in our lives. This work of reflection must be done, but "we cannot live our lives constantly looking back, listening back, lest we be turned to pillars of longing and regret."[1] As important as reflection may be, we must not live our lives looking over our shoulder. Because we live in the present, we should always be asking, "Where is God in the present moment? How do I meet the God of my past in the present?"

In traversing the pathway into the Mystery, we always live in the present moment. The secret to meeting God in the present lies in becoming aware. An old Christian master was visited by one of his disciples. On entering the room where the master sat in deep reflection, the disciple heard these questions: "As you approached the house, did you notice the firmness of the pavement beneath your feet? Were there birds in the trees? Did you hear the sound of the siren? How many steps were there leading up to the porch? Did you place your umbrella on the right or left side of the door? With which hand did you open the door?" The master's real question to the disciple was, "Are you aware?"

This concern for awareness in the present calls forth a number of challenging questions. How do we recognize the presence of God in the stuff of daily life? If by some gift we recognize the divine presence, what does that mean? If, indeed, God does come to us in the small happenings of everyday life and we perceive God's handiwork, how do we integrate this awareness into the ongoing flow of our lives?

These questions take the search for God out of the sanctuary and place it in the routine task of daily living. The spiritual giants of the past have always concerned themselves with the moment-by-moment, day-to-day living. Like them we ask, "How can we become contemporary with Christ, not in the ages gone by, not in the ages yet to come, but here and now?"

To begin to answer this question, recall the foundation of the spiritual journey. Our vision of God has been that the journey begins and ends in God. God is our contemporary, sustaining us during each moment of the journey. God intends to be enfleshed in us, to make the community of faith a re-presentation of God's Son and thus to make each of us participants in a living expression of God's will. God uses the routine events of every day—very ordinary acts such as rolling out of bed, eating, working at some task, having a conversation—to enflesh God's self in our lives.

How do we discern the uncommon presence of God in the common events of the day? Becoming aware of God's presence and participating with God create meaning in our personal lives and add to the larger story of history. This meaning, we believe, is preserved forever in the memory of God. Because of this eternal aspect of our choices, we take the search for the presence of God with total seriousness.

Imagine God at work in the ordinary events of your life and mine, creating meaning for us, for the whole

human story, and for God's self. You and I participate
in a project of cosmic significance! Our connection
comes in the occurrences of every day. An illustration
will help visualize this possibility. Several years ago the
Sunshine Skyway Bridge that arches the gulf from St.
Petersburg to Bradenton, Florida, was damaged by a
careless tugboat pilot. During reconstruction the bridge
was firmly anchored to the land on the St. Petersburg
side. The rebuilt portion of the bridge stretched out
over the water. Workers used steel and asphalt to extend the length of the bridge each day. When the con-
struction was complete, the bridge joined the two
pieces of land.

How does this bridge with its pilings, archways,
roadbeds, suspensions, and workers provide a model
for our consciousness of God in the moments of our
lives? The land on the St. Petersburg side represents the
original revelation of God as recorded in the Bible. The
pilings represent the continual breaking in of the Spirit
of God to provide support under the roadbed. The road-
way across the pilings symbolizes the continuing story
of meaning that is being created by those who work on
it. The workers are like the people of God living in obedience and thus extending God's story into the future.
The heavy steel cables that hold the sections of the
bridge represent the communion of the saints who
share with us in the creation of history. Those who
listen for God in the present moment and seek to respond to God's will are the workers doing the new con-
struction on the end of the bridge. The bridge arches
the chasm of time reaching from the past into the unknown future, and the bridge itself is the place for the
creation of meaning in the present moment.

Our lives share in the overarching purpose of God.
They have ultimate significance because we participate
in the creation of ultimate meaning. This magnificent
purpose of God incorporates our lives into a meaning
far greater than the pursuit of personal fulfillment, the

accumulation of wealth or power, or the gaining of personal recognition.

The Sacrament of the Present Moment

Some time ago an acquaintance recommended to me a book, *Abandonment to Divine Providence,* by Jean-Pierre de Caussade. Every page of the book repeats the message that God comes to us in the present moment, whether the content of the moment is pleasant or painful, joyous or sad. This spiritual guide impressed on me the startling truth that *everything,* every single occurrence in our lives, *must be greeted as the bearer of the presence of God.*

This very second, this beat of your heart, this moment of awareness presents you with the Divine Presence. Each moment forms a signal over which God broadcasts God's presence. To be fixed on the past, no matter how glorious, blinds us to the sacred invasion of the present. Straining our eyes looking for God in an uncreated future means that we leap over the reality of the divine here and now.

God is the God of now. Do not bail out on the present no matter how dull or painful. Be present to your own life, now. Attend to the movement of your life, here. Listen for the God who comes in the unfolding moments of this day. How tempted we are to vacate the present! We say, "If only I were someone else, if I were somewhere else, I would be happy and my life would have meaning." How diligently we try to escape the one certain moment, the present one! Will we ever learn to be who we are, where we are, doing the duty of the moment with the consciousness that this is God's appointment for us? This affirmation of the present does not mean that we are to sink into passivity in the midst of injustice. Rather, it suggests that all change begins with an acceptance of the present. In responding to God, begin where you are. Start with the present moment, for this moment contains the beginning of the path that leads to the will of God for you.

From the letters of Jean-Pierre de Caussade, I have gathered a number of rich metaphors of the present moment.[2] Each moment is:

• *A sacrament.* Each moment is the bread and wine mediating the presence of God to the receptive person.

• *A gift.* God gives earth, air, water, life, and in each of these God is given to us. God is present in the moment just as God is present in our breath, our food, and our sleep.

• *A veil.* While the moment carries the presence of God, it is a veiled presence. God is not visible to the naked eye; God is present only to faith. De Caussade says that God's word is given substance and visibility by the words, feelings, thoughts, and actions of the present moment.

• *A stone.* Each moment is a stone for building the house in which we live, or for extending the bridge of history. Each moment comes uncut and must be shaped for its proper place. To cast the moment away leaves a spot unfilled.

• *A mine.* The moment contains what we need. If we mine the wealth of the present moment, the next will provide what our life then requires.

• *A festival.* Each moment provides the food that we need to grow. If I can perceive it, this moment is indeed the banquet of God.

• *A communion with God.* This moment offers the medium for meeting God. When will we open ourselves to God, if not now? When will we fellowship with God, if not in the present moment?

• *The ocean's edge.* This present moment opens for us the sea of time that stretches out to eternity. The present moment links us with every future moment.

These metaphors of the moment reveal to us the possibilities immediately accessible to us in the present. Think about them. Write about them in your journal. Expand them until each enables you to celebrate the sacrament of the present moment.

Response to God in the Present Moment

How will we engage each sacred moment that manifests the will of God to us? How will we respond to God's call? We must face the moment with sensitivity because this call does not come with a label marked "God's will." Usually, the manifestation of the Spirit has a subtlety that will escape the careless glance.

The opportunity appears more like a small niche in the moment that only a gentle touch can stroke, or like a faint whisper only an attentive ear can hear. A friend comes to plan a meeting. Before the planning begins, the conversation turns to her need for spiritual direction. You forget the task at hand and respond to her immediate need. Is this perhaps the presence of God coming in the moment?

On a day when my calendar was more than full, an acquaintance stopped by my office to tell me about his plans for a career change. As he talked about his anticipation and his fears, I wondered with some irritation why he had come. I'm very busy, I thought to myself. Why is he telling me about this? Finally the awareness dawned: God had appointed me his minister for the moment. Do you see the difference this perception makes?

There can be no screening of the moment, no direction of providence by our own willpower. We cannot prefabricate the moments. We can choose the will of God only as it comes to us in all these incarnate forms. As we choose, as we respond to God's will, we become part of the great incarnation project of God. God is incarnated in human history through the conscious re-

sponse of God's people—incarnation by participation.
"Be it unto me according to your word," said Mary. By
participation we share in the eternal life of God and the
creation of meaning in history.

But the human response must be in the moment. The
moment appears, then disappears, and with it the opportunity that existed. De Caussade says, "What was
the best thing for us to do in the moment that has
passed is no longer so, for the will of God is now manifesting itself in those circumstances which are the duty
of the present moment."[3]

What is the meaning of life but obedience to the will
of God? Obedience to God in the moment must be
valued above every other act, even above prayer and
worship. What God wills for you, whether it is the simple act of cleaning house or writing a letter or reading
a book—that is the one thing necessary for you.

How does a serious person know what God wills? Too
many fanatics have claimed to be guided by God only
to be lost in their own illusions. I recall a man who spoke
to me after a worship service. He declared that I had
spoken the Word of God to the people. He himself had
been called of God to witness to this congregation, but
no one would listen. He also was certain that God had
called him to become the governor of the state. Persons
like him, obsessed with their own importance, make us
fearful of believing that God can indeed speak to us in
the events of our lives.

Will we permit the misguided to rob us of the presence that offers itself to us? The biblical story unfolds
the character of God. In it we discover God's will. As we
become acquainted with God, we begin to know what
God desires. Keith Miller illustrates this idea: "When
you were a child, if you had stolen a pair of skates from
a neighbor, do you know what your father would have
said?" Of course, each of us does. In many instances our
father is dead, but we still know what he would have
said because we knew his character. When we learn
God's story, we begin to absorb an understanding of

God's nature. When we are confronted with choices in the present moment, we know what God would do because we have become deeply acquainted with God's nature and God's will.

As the truth of God's will appears in each moment, it will always have the character of Christ. Christ is the will of God made visible. Turn to Christ. In each moment Christ wills to reproduce his quality of life in you. He wills to actualize love—agape love—in your choices. No form of that love will ever be forced on you. God offers you the freedom to make your own response to the dynamic moment. When you do choose Christ, in that exact instant God becomes incarnate in your history. God's will is done; God's kingdom comes.

But how can such a life be lived with freedom, abandon, and spontaneity? How can the Spirit be liberated and not enslaved in human striving? To do God's will in the moment fulfills us and fulfills the purpose of God simultaneously. Embracing that will, letting it work its purpose in us, permitting it to guide us toward destiny, even grasping it with our active response propels us down the pathway toward our ultimate fulfillment.

The will of God appears in the contrived as well as the unpremeditated events of our lives. Some events appear to be the result of our careful planning. We decide to go shopping. We plan an outing. Or we decide to set aside an hour for God. We arise and depart to face the tasks of the day. All these events seem to arise from human initiative. And yet the will of God appears in these very events. Even in the humdrum of life, God's will lies waiting to be recognized. The substance of our life's meaning hides there, waiting to be grasped by faith.

This life-fulfilling will offers itself in the form of unpremeditated occurrences. Like a chance visitor, the unexpected communication comes to us. A friend calls, a stranger visits, a motorist stops to let off a passenger, a seeker for God shows no desire to leave, the doctor insists on your losing weight, an illness stops all activity, a loved one dies—through such occurrences God is presented to us.

Consider two symbols for God's will. A straightedge ruler lays out a single course from which we must not deviate. Those who serve God by following a set of rules are like those who adopt the straightedge as a symbol for the will of God. On the other hand, a magnet also symbolizes an approach to the will of God. A magnet sends forth an invisible, attracting force. As children, most of us performed the science experiment of putting a magnet under a sheet of paper holding metal shavings, then watching the effect that moving the magnet had on the metal. The magnet draws, lures, compels the metal to come to it. If the metal substance suddenly became animate, it would say that it feels attracted to the magnet; it would even feel itself gliding toward the power exerted on it. When it reached the magnet, it would be held and sustained by this strange but forceful attraction.

Is not the will of God a magnet in every event of our life? Unlike the metal shavings, we humans have been created with a craving for God. God therefore works through the hunger in our spirit, whose restlessness compels us to search for fulfillment.

Love defines the will of God in the moment. Jesus said, "You shall love the Lord your God with all your heart, and with all your soul, and with all your mind. This is the great and first commandment. And a second is like it, You shall love your neighbor as yourself" (Matt. 22:37–38). Obedience to love will reshape life's boundaries. As smoke rising from burning logs changes in form and direction with the wind, even so our circumstances change the shape of love.

Our search for this mysterious will causes us to continue asking, "What is the will of God for us in the present moment? How do we respond to it?" The will of God always shows itself in the duties of everyday life. Not in another place, not in a different vocation, not in the context of self-chosen relationships, but *here* where

God has placed us. *Now,* in this unfolding moment, God's unique will for us presents itself. Duty does not mean drudgery, like the tasks imposed by a demanding parent. Our peculiar responsibilities in our present situation—these are the duties of the moment.

These duties have many faces and equally as many forms. Take the parent/child relationship as one model. Children must obey their parents, a duty made clear by God. Parents are to love their children, a duty likewise made clear. The command of God does not make clear the many forms this obedience and love may take. Both parent and child must choose the particular form of response. One child obeys the parental command reluctantly, while another obeys joyfully. One may reject parental suggestions, only to accept them later. In like fashion, love takes many shapes—a benevolent, forgiving love; a compliant, permissive love; a demanding, tough love. Obedience to duty points us in the proper direction, but it does not inhibit us.

The will of God for some may be in the accomplishment of extraordinary achievements. If it is God's will for some persons to achieve much, they must do that. To refuse to actualize their gifts, to turn from the opportunity to create, to achieve, or to affect the lives of great masses of persons would be disobedience to God's will.

God's will for others may be the simple, routine performance of ordinary tasks. In this instance it would be disobedience for such persons to seek greatness.

If we should compare these two groups, the ones who respond to the simple duties of everyday life and the ones who respond to some extraordinary call of God, which pleases God more? Which has the fulfilled life? Both! In both cases persons are doing God's will, and that is all that matters.

But how will the person with an extraordinary duty recognize this special call of God? A special call enters our awareness quietly, unobtrusively. At first the thought may be repugnant, perhaps even frightening.

But it refuses to go away. Again and again, like an
uninvited guest, it knocks at the door seeking admission
into our life.

A special call of God does not go away, and with its
persistent tug at our mind and heart comes an eventual
familiarity and a loss of fear. We recognize that God is
calling a part of ourself that may have been lost or
unrecognized, a potential aspect waiting to be called
forth. Such recognition leads to a deeper discovery of
self and of God's will.

Where will this new idea take us? That question finds
its resolution in the act of obedience. In keeping with
our journey metaphor, God's special call invites us to
risk leaving the safety and security of home to travel to
parts unknown. Propelled by the magnetic quality of
God's will, we set out, ready to realize that when we
embrace the will of God, we grasp the power that fulfills
our lives, the aim of human history, and the eternal
purpose of Almighty God.

A Way of Reflecting on the Day

To what can we compare a life that expects the presence of God in the ordinary events of life? The presence
of God is like a child's puzzle in which a string of letters
fills the page with no spaces between the words. The
puzzle challenges the child to separate the letters into
complete words and discover the message hidden
there. On the spiritual journey we must identify the
hidden words in the events of our lives, separate them,
and punctuate them to gather the meaning of our life.

We can begin this task by dividing the day into para-
graphs of meaning. In *To Will God's Will* we used a
similar procedure to identify the different legs of the
journey. In this instance we are working with hours
rather than years.

A friend of mine introduced me to this way of reflecting on the lived moments of the day by showing me how
to shift to a focus on consciousness. He encouraged me

to ask important questions like: What is occurring in my consciousness each day? How is God manifest to me during the course of the day? Taking his suggestion, I developed a way to listen for God in the events of the day.

This way of reflecting on a day has been one approach I have used in an effort to discern the activity of God in my life. It has heightened my sensitivity to the Spirit in the day I am living. In some instances I have been able to discern God's will in the midst of a situation and respond to it. I do not wish to convey the impression that I am able every hour of the day to live in this consciousness of God. I can't. I don't. But this experience has greatly heightened my awareness.

You could spend an hour with each of the steps in the process. Some days I go through the entire list; on other days I select three or four aspects for reflection. (See the exercise for chapter 3 in Appendix A.)

I looked through my journal for an illustration of how I have fleshed out this exercise. Here is one I found, with my added comments in parentheses.

(The segments of the day: April 21)

1. An early run
2. Breakfast with a friend
3. Had idea to give a book to the Columbia Friendship Circle (a group from the Women of the Church)
4. Assisted my pastor in the creation of a new stewardship program for my church
5. Brief statement to the Columbia Friendship Circle and the presentation of my booklet, "An Adventure in Prayer"
6. Meeting with the CTS Press board
7. Explored the use of videotape with denomination leaders
8. Quiet evening at home
9. A forgotten dream
10. Fasted the day

Prayer of Illumination

*O God, as I reflect on my life of yesterday, enable me
to see the movement of your Spirit and the unity of the
events of my life.*

(After identifying the data of my life, I reviewed the
flow of the day. Reading over the phrases I had written,
I closed my eyes and pictured myself reliving the day.
The day felt lively and full of meaning. Not every day
feels that way. Some feel flat, even painful. I paused to
give thanks to God. For the events of April 21 my
thanksgivings were:)

*Thank you for the cool, invigorating air I experienced
in running. Thanks for the release of tension and the
refreshing feeling when I have finished.*

*Thank you for my friend Tap Hanson, a companion on
the journey for a long time. I am glad to offer him my
friendship today because he has been so generous with
his through the years. Thank you for his search for
spiritual maturity.*

*Thank you for J. Davison Philips and his willingness
for me to give each member of the Columbia Friendship
Circle a copy of my booklet.*

*I am grateful to you for the creative energy I felt when
my pastor and I began to design the stewardship program. I had never thought of grounding stewardship in
baptism before.*

*Thank you for the CTS Press board and for creating
an atmosphere of understanding and trust.*

*Thanks for my conversation with the denominational
leaders regarding the use of video in teaching. Be present to them as they help me understand how to use the
medium.*

(Following the reliving of the day in thanksgiving, I
looked for the broken places in my life that require
confession.)

In my presentation to the Columbia Friendship Circle, I really blew it. I got caught up in promoting the booklet rather than presenting its content and purpose. My ego got in the way of your Spirit. I'm sorry.

In my conversation with my pastor about stewardship, I felt so much creative energy. I had an explosion of ideas and felt so expansive as they flowed freely. But, I had to call attention to the ideas—to how unique and good they are. I really lost control of myself and pride overcame me. I regret that I idolized myself and my gifts instead of giving thanks to you. I hope to be more sensitive to the source of my creativity next time.

I'm not aware of any other breaks in my relationship with you yesterday. I trust that this day will be lived in your presence.

(After my confession, I sought to integrate the day into the total flow of my life. The questions that I raised: How do the events of April 21 fit into the movement of my life? What clues do I see for my future? What themes were repeated in my life yesterday?)

One theme of yesterday that seems to be a part of my total life: maintaining good health. Both running and fasting keep my blood pressure down. As I get older, I am more conscious of my need to reduce stress, rest more, and watch my diet.

My breakfast with Tap Hanson adds to a long relationship of love and trust stretching over twenty years.

I spent time searching for quiet, an important quest these days.

Being fifty-one years old, I expect to be a mentor to persons. In fact, some who once guided me now look to me for support.

Four of the events of my life had to do with entrepreneurship: my meeting with my pastor, my distributing books to the ladies, my meeting with the CTS Press board, and my meeting with the denominational leaders. All these encounters related to creating and dis-

tributing new things. Activities such as these have been part of my life for the past twenty years.

In all of these experiences I felt happy, intrigued, fulfilled. But I so often lack control over my productive drive. I do not wish to have my inspirations run away from me undisciplined and unformed. My call for the time being seems to be in teaching, creating, and distributing resources to churches. In fulfilling this call, I must not destroy myself physically, nor forget the source of my energy, gifts, imagination, and creativity.

This reflection on April 21 illustrates how I try to examine the message of the day. It is an examination of consciousness for that day. You might also call it a contemplation of the day before God. This intensive reflection results in the recognition of the presence of God in the events of the day; it provides a way of confession and cleansing that keeps your life open to God; it offers you a way of reentering events, viewing them intentionally, and "seeing" what was happening in encounters. Reflecting on the day draws together its meaning for the moment and also preserves it more distinctly in your memory. As you place several days of reflection like this together, you will see more themes reoccurring, and the sense of movement in your life becomes readily discernible.

Do not make the reflection on the day a laborious task. Neither should you feel compelled to reflect on your life like this every day. Let this be one of the adventures of the spiritual journey.

The exercise for chapter 3 in Appendix A will guide you in reflecting on the events of your day.

4

Journey to the Desert

*In the desert journeyers listen
to the silent whispers of God.*

At every stage of the spiritual journey, each of us will be invited by the Spirit into the form of prayer most appropriate for us. The first pathway into the Mystery may be meditation with its use of words and reason; then contemplation through images; at another time the Spirit will open our eyes to the Divine Presence in the events of the day. A new way of prayer presents itself to us as familiar ways grow dull and fruitless. The stage of the journey, the type of personality, the exposure to models—all these influence the sequence and the timing of the kind of prayer most needed in our lives.

Often the most difficult prayer is the emptying form—a wordless, imageless prayer disclosed through silence. The travelers to the sacred center give this road many names. Some speak of the way as silence, others as solitude or contemplation, and still others call it the desert. Whatever the way, it leads in the opposite direction from activity, effort, speaking. This way calls us to stillness, waiting before God to hear the voice of silence. The silence speaks a language that cannot be heard in the haste of life.

The biblical writers knew this way. Habakkuk said, "The LORD is in his holy temple; let all the earth keep silence before him" (Hab. 2:20). The psalmist spoke the Lord's word, "Be still, and know that I am God" (Ps. 46:10).

Recall the experience of Elijah. He had defeated the prophets of Baal. In the euphoria of his victory, Jezebel declared that she would do to him what he had done to her prophets: have him put to death. Distraught, Elijah fled into the wilderness and sat depressed under the juniper tree. The Lord provided him with nourishment and then sent him to Horeb, the mount of God. Elijah made his home in a cave for forty days of fasting and prayer, after which God came to him.

> And [God] said, "Go forth, and stand upon the mount before the LORD." And behold, the LORD passed by, and a great and strong wind rent the mountains, and broke in pieces the rocks before the LORD, but the LORD was not in the wind; and after the wind an earthquake, but the LORD was not in the earthquake; and after the earthquake a fire, but the LORD was not in the fire; and *after the fire a still small voice. And when Elijah heard it, he wrapped his face in his mantle and went out and stood at the entrance of the cave.* . . . And the LORD said to him, "Go, return on your way to the wilderness of Damascus." (1 Kings 19:11–13, 15; italics added)

In the wilderness Elijah met himself; in the wilderness he heard the voice of God!

A journey into the desert will help you begin to discover your need for inner quiet. There you will meet pilgrims who have made their way to the desert; they will show the way to inner silence. This way to the center, though frightening to some, leads to a sanctuary of the Spirit where God speaks unutterable words.

Our Need for Silence

The silence of a symphony hall just before the conductor's downbeat would never be chosen as a symbol for our everyday lives. Just recall an average day in your life, such as yesterday. My average day went like this:

Arise at 6 A.M.

Quick breakfast, coffee.

Drive to work on busy Clairmont Road.

These noises implode on my ears: horns blowing, motors running, shouts of children, a plane flying over.

At the office: A student drops in. The telephone rings. My secretary interrupts with a question. The telephone rings again.

All day these sounds invade the silence with interruption and distraction.

Return home at 6 P.M. Bite of dinner. A little work around the house. An hour of television. To bed.

The noises of one twenty-four-hour period are like the constant interruptions of an airline agent announcing the departure of another flight every two or three minutes. Life is like that, full of noise and distraction.

Because our days are filled with waves of sound, we must make a serious effort to find a place within ourselves which is quiet, serene, a haven beyond the noise pollution of the day. Is there such a point in each of us, hidden beneath the surface noise? Can all of us, even novices, find it? Can we endure the anxiety of silence long enough to encounter this deep place within?

To enter the silence requires that we consciously monitor the entry between the inner world of quiet and the external world of distraction. Silence requires a guard at the doorway of our minds. "The enemy of attentive listening is extraneous noise, both the externally generated and the internally generated kinds," says Urban Holmes.[1] An effective monitor must eliminate the noise from beneath as well as the noise from the outside. The former may be harder to erase.

This search for silence leads us to a center within, a still point at which our attention can be focused on God. At this point we listen not for words, or for images. We await the touch of reality on our awareness, a receptivity to the naked presence of God. Nothing to say, no request to make, no new truth to receive—just being in the presence of God.

At the still point we must learn the language of silence. There we hear the unspoken whispers of God. In the quiet depths the unuttered word of God surrounds us, searching for an opening to penetrate the core of our being. The silence opens us to the mystery of the great eternal God. The mystery, unnamed, possesses us, conditions our being.

Henri Nouwen recounts a story about silence told by a Taoist philosopher.

> The purpose of a fish trap is to catch fish and when the fish are caught, the trap is forgotten. The purpose of a rabbit snare is to catch rabbits. When the rabbits are caught, the snare is forgotten. The purpose of the word is to convey ideas. When the ideas are grasped, the words are forgotten. Where can I find a man who has forgotten words?[2]

The man who has forgotten words could help us learn the meaning of silence.

I have never met the person who has forgotten words, nor have I met one who knows fully the communicative power of the sacred silence. I myself have never been to the center of the "still point," but I have been to its edge and there I glimpsed the possibility of union with God. At the edge I felt peace, the peace of reconciliation with myself and with God. I came near enough to the center to feel a hunger for the union of my spirit with God and, on returning from the silence, I have experienced God's presence incarnate at the core of my being. God's presence becomes real without debate; we encounter reality itself. Only in the silence does our personal journey get firmly grounded in a conscious relationship with God. Surely you, just as I, feel a hunger for God. If we do not hunger for God's presence, we will never experience the depths of contemplative prayer.

Jesus' Discovery of Silence

Jesus began his ministry with a protracted period of silence, forty days alone in the desert. Recall the account according to Matthew:

> Then Jesus was led up by the Spirit into the wilderness to be tempted by the devil. And he fasted forty days and forty nights, and afterward he was hungry. And the tempter came and said to him, "If you are the Son of God, command these stones to become loaves of bread." But he answered, "It is written, 'Man shall not live by bread alone, but by every word that proceeds from the mouth of God.'"
>
> Then the devil took him to the holy city, and set him on the pinnacle of the temple, and said to him, "If you are the Son of God, throw yourself down; for it is written, 'He will give his angels charge of you,' and 'On their hands they will bear you up, lest you strike your foot against a stone.'" Jesus said to him, "Again it is written, 'You shall not tempt the Lord your God.'" Again, the devil took him to a very high mountain, and showed him all the kingdoms of the world and the glory of them; and he said to him, "All these I will give you, if you will fall down and worship me." Then Jesus said to him, "Begone, Satan! for it is written, 'You shall worship the Lord your God and him only shall you serve.'" Then the devil left him, and behold, angels came and ministered to him. (Matthew 4:1–11)

What can we learn from Jesus' search for silence? First, note that the Spirit led Jesus into the desert. This hunger for silence did not originate with our Lord; he was not seeking to earn favor with God. The desire for this solitary communion with God must be initiated by the Spirit of God, not by curiosity or by efforts to impress God or other people. The Holy Spirit creates the hunger for God and gives both the courage and the strength to enter the desert.

In the desert Jesus began a fast. A fast calls for self-denial. We turn away from the good things in creation in order to give attention to something better—the Creator, God. All God's gifts to us are right and good, but in periods of intense response to the Spirit we sacrifice these to live our obedience to God more fully. When we turn from legitimate human hungers such as food, sex, and other people, we are left only with ourselves. In this aloneness we are face to face with God. Even in our day, the practice of refraining from food, sex, and contact with other persons for an hour, a day, or a week attunes us to God.

In the desert Jesus had only God. No crowds to address, no pressing needs to meet, no accusers to fend off, no disciples to teach: only God. In the desert Jesus heard the sounds of nature—the howl of a jackal, the song of a bird, the scraping of sand under his sandals and the scuff of his foot against a stone—but these sounds of nature blended with the silence and mediated to him the awareness of God. Somewhere there is a symbolic desert place for each of us where we, too, can retreat from the rush, the noise, and the complexity of life to meet the God of the depths.

In the desert Jesus had met both the devil and the angels. The desert provided his most severe test—food, pride, and greed, the greatest perversions of human nature—and Jesus mastered them all. We will meet angels and demons too. The Desert Fathers, who lived in the Egyptian desert during the fourth and fifth centuries, said that each person has a demon to test and an angel to protect and succor. Beneath the surface lurk those fears we cannot face, the questions about ourselves we had rather not answer. The silence opens the door to their prison; they appear unbidden and demand recognition.

But in the silence we also encounter our unnamed angels. We discover sources of strength never before recognized. The pervasive awareness of God that occurs in the silence provides an unshakable security. The word of love spoken to us heals and guides and empowers.

The desert conditioned Jesus' understanding of his

ministry. He made every important decision in the environment of prayer by retreating to the memory of the desert where he learned to listen to God.

Before he chose the twelve apostles, he spent all night in prayer (Luke 6:12).

At the news of John the Baptist's death, he drew apart to a lonely place (Matt. 14:13).

After feeding the 5,000, he sent his disciples away, dismissed the crowd, and "went up into the hills by himself to pray" (Matt. 14:23).

He prayed before ministry. "And in the morning, a great while before day, he rose and went out to a lonely place, and there he prayed" (Mark 1:35).

After the twelve returned from their mission, Jesus said to them, "Come away by yourselves to a lonely place" (Mark 6:31). He taught them the value of silence in their ministry.

After healing a leper, Jesus "withdrew to the wilderness and prayed" (Luke 5:16). Solitude renews and replenishes the spirit in the life of God's servant.

Jesus went up into a mountain to find strength for his journey to the cross (Matt. 17:1–9).

In preparation for his holiest of work, Jesus sought the solitude of the garden in Gethsemane. There he prayed, "Not my will, but thine be done" (Matt. 26:36–46).

If Jesus required a retreat to the desert, not just once but over and over again, how much more do we need to isolate minutes, hours, maybe days, for a desert experience?

A few years ago I went to the seminary chapel at the hour of daily worship. Arriving early, I sat quietly in prayer. "What would you say to me, Lord?" I asked.

Quickly the reply came, "Go, sell what you have, give the money to the poor, then come and follow me."

"Wait a minute," I retorted.

The voice would not go away. "Go . . . sell . . . give . . . come . . . follow." Imperatives that demanded obedience.

Ever since that call broke the silence, I have been troubled. What does God mean: Am I literally to sell all? Or am I to be willing to sell all? Could this symbolize my call to the desert?

I have not finished listening to this word. Regularly, it calls me to examine my loyalties and my priorities.

The Desert for Us

Serious journeyers even in our day find their desert, a place of retreat where they can practice their silence. One of the first persons I encountered who spoke of the silence was priest and author Henri Nouwen. Like many of us, he was immersed in the world of noise and heavy demands. He spoke a great deal about prayer and the need for silence but found little of it himself.

Through the years he found his hunger for silence growing until he could no longer ignore it. During this period of preparation he had met a spiritual guide at a monastery in Kentucky. This guide later became the abbot of the Abbey of the Genesee in upstate New York. After several visits with this spiritual director, Nouwen requested permission to live as a monk for seven months. In half a year permission was granted.

As he contemplated seven months of silence in a monastic setting, Nouwen realized that his life was filled with paradoxes, many of them the same paradoxes that will confront us as we search for our silence:

> While complaining about too many demands, I felt uneasy when none were made. While speaking about the burden of letter writing, an empty mailbox made me sad. While fretting about tiring lecture tours, I felt disappointed when there were no invitations. While speaking nostalgically about an empty desk, I feared the day on which that would come true. In short: while desiring to be alone, I was frightened of being left alone. The more I became aware of these paradoxes, the more I started to see how much I had indeed fallen in love with my own

compulsions and illusions, and how much I needed to step back and wonder, "Is there a quiet stream underneath the fluctuating affirmations and rejections of my little world? Is there a still point where my life is anchored and from which I can reach out with hope and courage and confidence?"[3]

What compulsions and illusions would we find if we were to step back from the rush of our lives? The silence gives us space to do that, to look at the way we live and to find the courage to make new decisions.

The encounter with silence at the Abbey of the Genesee continues to influence Nouwen's thought and ministry. Several years later he described his experience of engaging the silence:

> In solitude I get rid of my scaffolding: no friends to talk with, no telephone calls to make, no meetings to attend, no music to entertain, no books to distract, just me— naked, vulnerable, weak, sinful, deprived, broken— nothing. It is this nothingness that I have to face in my solitude, a nothingness so dreadful that everything in me wants to run to my friends, my work, and my distractions so that I can forget my nothingness and make myself believe that I am worth something.[4]

Is it possible that this engagement with the silence could provide us with a new center for our life? A new source of energy? A clarifying of the meaning of our life? Maybe we should begin thinking about finding our desert!

One day while flipping through a publisher's catalog I saw the heading "Spirituality," a subject that has always intrigued me, and the title *Letters from the Desert*. Though I had never heard of the author, my curiosity was awakened, and I ordered the book. When I began to read it, I knew at once that this man was destined to play a major role in this period of my life.

Brother Carlo described his call to the desert. A Roman Catholic layman, he had been an activist until age forty-four. At that time he felt a call to the desert, literally. In response to the call he left everything to spend ten years in the desert listening to God.

Brother Carlo reports that the voice making the call said to him, "Leave everything and come with me into the desert. It is not your acts and deeds that I want; I want your prayer, your love."[5]

My initial conviction about his role in my life deepened as Brother Carlo fed my soul with profound insights into the nature of God. Images, metaphors, and word pictures leaped from every page. After I had read this book, I had to order every book he had written, sit at his feet, and listen to his visits with God in the desert.

As I read, it seemed that he had looked into the face of God and reproduced that vision in words. By some magic or mystery the words he wrote became transparent, and I could see God through his eyes. Brother Carlo commends the desert to all of us:

> When one speaks of the soul's desert, and says that the desert must be present in your life, you must not think only of the Sahara or the desert of Judea, or into the High Valley of the Nile.
>
> Certainly it is not everyone who can have the advantage of being able to carry out in practice this detachment from daily life. The Lord conducted me into the real desert because I was so thick-skinned. For me, it was necessary. But all that sand was not enough to erase the dirt from my soul, even the fire was not enough to remove the rust from Ezekiel's pot.
>
> But the same way is not for everybody. And if you cannot go into the desert, you must nonetheless "make some desert" in your life. Every now and then leaving men and looking for solitude to restore, in prolonged silence and prayer, the stuff of your soul. This is the meaning of "desert" in your spiritual life.
>
> One hour a day, one day a month, eight days a year, for longer if necessary, you must leave everything and everybody and retire, alone with God. . . .
>
> But the desert is not the final stopping place. It is a

stage on the journey. Because, as I told you, our vocation is contemplation in the streets. . . .

You must go back among men, mix with them, live your intimacy with God in the noise of their cities. It will be difficult but you must do it. And for this the grace of God will not fail you.[6]

Nor will the grace of God fail us. In our small desert we will discover a fountain of grace that waters the relationships of every day. That grace refreshes our souls but also flows through us to silence the noise of the streets.

A contemporary of mine, Hal Edwards, Executive Director of the Christian Laity of Chicago, told me about his week-long retreat at Well Spring, the retreat center of the Church of the Savior in Washington, D.C. I inquired at length how such an experience could help a modern person find a deep silence. I asked him to tell me candidly about his eight days of silence with fasting. Hal reported:

Since I am such an extrovert, entering into the silence felt like leprosy; it frightened me to the core of my being. The first few days were particularly traumatic. I experienced headaches, anxiety, and boredom. These feelings dominated my consciousness for the first three days.

After three days, however, I found myself entering into a new depth of consciousness. I began to experience a union with nature I had never known before. I saw birds and bushes and sunsets as though for the first time. Nature became personalized as we communed together as creatures of God.

I found myself restless; I wanted to read; I felt an urge to produce. I'm such a compulsive. In ten days I once wrote one hundred and eighty-six pages in my journal. Early on, I found it virtually impossible to just "be."

As the days progressed, I began to settle into the silence. I found myself entering into a new place with God. During my descent into the depths, two phrases kept coming to my mind which symbolized my experience:

"wasting time with God" and "the palace of nowhere." These phrases helped me to become more friendly to the silence.

During the eight days I spoke daily with my spiritual guide for about thirty minutes; the remainder of the day I spent in silence. In the extended silence I came to the center of my own darkness. I encountered my emptiness before God. The experience of this void filled me with terror.

One night during this journey inward I had a startling and revealing dream. I dreamed that a man came to my cabin and rapped on the door. I awakened from sleep certain that someone was knocking at my door. When I went to the door, no one was there.

The next day I told the dream to my spiritual guide, who suggested that in my journal I write a dialogue with this wisdom figure from my deep mind. As I wrote an imaginative dialogue with this figure, I discovered that the visitor was no stranger to me; he had been with me all of my life. He knew me better than I knew myself.

As the days slipped by, I came to a place of rest. At the center of my being I found a still point, a place of solitude in the presence of God. In that place I began to feel that I had come home to myself. Like birds migrating home, I had passed through all the layers of my being to arrive at my place of origin. I was finally at home with myself.

During the retreat I had a number of dreams. My unconscious seemed to be working overtime. While I fasted and centered in the silence, that tiny membrane which separates the deeper mind from consciousness became thinner and dozens of images poured through in dreams. I wrote all of these in my journal for later reflection.

Simple things spoke powerfully to me in this desert time. I discovered a tiny white rock that I contemplated for hours. After investing so much of myself in this small rock, it became a symbol of the silence for me. More than anything else from this experience I came to cherish the silence. Wisdom, I believe, comes out of silence.

When I returned from the desert, I felt very aware of persons, more than I could ever remember. I had a keen perception of the needs and desires of my family. I came home to listen rather than tell what I had experienced. The memory of those eight days felt too sacred to relate to anyone at the time. I needed to live my way into their meaning. Assimilating that experience has taken months, maybe years.

When I hit the streets to continue my work, I experienced daily a severe noise shock. Yet, in the silence I had found a center to which I could return. That little desert within helped me recover a sense of peace, a knowledge of the presence of God.

Anyone who makes this journey to the center of the self needs a spiritual guide to walk alongside. The guide not only provides companionship and support but direction through the dark tunnels. I would not wish to see anyone set out on this voyage alone.

This report from the silence provides glimpses into what an experience of the silence might mean to any one of us. Keep in mind, however, that everyone has his or her own journey to make. Whether the reporter is Nouwen, Carretto, or Edwards, these only bear witness to their experience. Your experience will have its own distinctive marks. Whether this desert takes the form of the literal desert of Brother Carlo or the symbolic desert of a fast, a retreat, or a few hours alone, each of us needs to know how to engage the silence and listen to its utterance. A few suggestions may be of help on your journey into the desert.

Entering the Silence

A trip to the desert, whether for a brief or an extended time, requires a call. This call comes in the form of a longing, a hunger for the unity of life, a desire to understand the purpose of life, a longing for wholeness, for a deeper relation with God.

The call often begins with a new awareness of our potentiality. Sometimes the cry comes from the depths, "There must be more to life than I have experienced."

The call may come through the witness of another.

My own awakening came that way. I had never thought of going to the desert for an extended period until I read *Letters from the Desert*. Something in Carretto's witness gripped me. I do not know if I will ever make it to the Sahara, but I have a hunger for the silence. I question myself; "Do I have the courage to be in the desert for even a week? Could I bear the silence, the loss of everything but God?" I don't know. I have a restless curiosity that I suspect will one day lead me to my own desert.

The very thought of taking eight days alone as Hal Edwards did seems a distant possibility for most of us; we could possibly manage a day or two at best. To achieve any consistency, we will probably have to settle for an hour every day or two.

Whether or not I make it to the literal desert, I must now find a place in my busy life to label "desert." My desert is now a corner of the room, sometimes a cottage at the beach, or a house in the mountains. The desert is often a day at the monastery.

Once you have found your desert place, you will need a simple plan to structure your time. Without a notion of how to use your silence, even a day feels interminable. A good friend of mine unexpectedly popped into town on a scheduled retreat day and I asked him to go along.

"What are we going to do all day?" he asked.

"Pray."

"Pray? All day?" He explained that it did not take him that long to pray.

On the way to the retreat center at the monastery, I talked with him about a structure for the day. Together we worked out a simple plan for the time we had. Then each of us took separate rooms and spent the day alone. The time sped by. On the way home my friend reflected, "I didn't get nearly finished with my prayers. I completed about half of what we had planned. I have never spent such a short day in my life."

Time flies in the desert.

As you structure your day, begin with the outer world. Take a walk. Pay attention to the physical world—trees, bushes, grass, birds, a rock. Give your attention to the order of creation.

You will make an important discovery by paying attention to something very small and insignificant. Focus on a rock, an ant, a tiny vine struggling for life, or a duck swimming on the pond. Spend time contemplating this piece of creation. It is a medium for the voice of God. In the silence listen to what God says through creation.

After a period of reflection on the outside world, retire into your inner world. Find a quiet place: a room, a spot in the woods, a garden. Begin by letting your body come to rest. Permit every muscle of your body to relax.

Your breathing can help you become quiet. Count your breaths. See if you can count ten breaths without permitting your mind to wander even one time. This focus on breathing relaxes your body and clears your mind.

Speak to each part of your body. Tell it to relax. Begin with your toes. Move next to your foot and proceed until you have spoken to every part of your body. When you reach your head, you will feel a deep relaxation throughout your body.

I have found the image of warm water rising over my body in a tub to be relaxing. Imagine that you are sitting in a tub that is filling with warm water. Think of the water rising inch by inch until it covers your whole body. Don't worry if you go to sleep; you needed the rest.

Whatever method you use for getting there, in the relaxed silence let your mind become receptive to the Spirit of God. Listen to what God says. God will speak through the ideas that leap into your consciousness. Where do you think ideas come from, anyway?

When you come to silence, give your undivided attention to God. Experiencing the silence does not require words or thoughts or feelings. You, a tiny creature before so great and loving a God, offer your naked self to God. That offer of awareness is all. It is enough.

There will be times, possibly many times, when nothing happens in the silence. At least, nothing happens that you can describe to anyone. Yet in that indescribable silence God grasps your spirit and transforms it in ways that no one can explain. We go to the desert; we come back; we cannot tell anyone very much of what has happened. Yet we are different because we have been touched by God.

Expectations in the Desert

Do not place any great expectations on your trip to the desert. Receive what God offers you. Go to the desert to listen to God.

Whatever God provides in the desert will heal, direct, and enrich your life. You will hear what you most need. It may even be that God will say nothing to you. If that is what God chooses, so be it.

When I have introduced persons to a short desert experience, most have been gratified with what they have seen and heard. Here are a few reports:

> "I discovered rather forcefully that I like myself. To be alone with myself is a privilege that I exercise so little."

> "I loved it! I loved not only the things that I discovered in nature on the outside but the things I found on the inside. Some of the things that I found on the inside are the very things that keep me from the silence."

> "In my silence, I was flooded with memories of significant people in my life. I got glimpses of what the silence could mean to me."

> "I found a quiet place amid a patch of blooming yellow flowers. I sat down. I looked at the flowers. I was conscious of the birds chirping and the wind blowing. This felt like the place for me, my place. I had a supreme sense of 'being.'
> "I studied the trees. The leaves became symbols of God's unique creativity. I sat down on a rock. I saw a tiny vine struggling to make its way across the rock. Over my

shoulder I saw a stunted, deformed tree that had been beaten down by the wind. I thought, God made that tree and has preserved it through all of its struggles. Will he not do the same for me?"

"When the time was up, I did not want to come back."

Whatever else may occur, I suspect that when you go to the desert, you will discover a fire, one that will warm your whole being. Others will both see and feel the warmth. On occasion strangers from the cold will gather to be warmed by the heat from your fire. Often you will be unable to identify the divine activity. Maybe it is best that you do not. You do not go to the desert to make yourself feel better or to become more useful; you go to the desert to meet God, however God becomes known to you.

If your path leads to the desert, follow it. No other way will advance your journey.

The exercise for chapter 4 in Appendix A offers some key questions to help you reflect on your experience of silence. Answer them fully in your journal.

5

Spiritual Companionship on the Journey

Even those who can see will benefit from an experienced guide.

The various pathways into the Mystery may have as many dangers as the road from Jerusalem down to Jericho, a journey infested with robbers and murderers. Hal Edwards's report on his descent into the depths indicated the perilous terrain over which the journeyer travels and carried with it the recommendation of a spiritual director who knows the landscape of the soul and the dark places the journeyer encounters. But a spiritual director can serve a person's growth at other times and in a variety of ways.

In these precarious days serious journeyers need direction for their growth. Since many of the traditional landmarks have eroded, blurring the way to God, a spiritual guide will save us from endless wanderings.

My ideas on spiritual companionship grow out of my own need for help and thus have the character of witness. By sharing my search for a spiritual guide, I hope to answer four questions for you: What is a spiritual companion? What are the essential qualities a spiritual companion needs? How does the relationship begin? And what are the values of this relationship?

My awareness of spiritual guidance began more than ten years ago. A fellow minister who was laboring with me on an experimental project at the Institute of

Church Renewal unexpectedly asked me, "To whom are you accountable?" Though his question took me by surprise, I responded with a degree of vain delight, "To no one but God!" I mistakenly feared that accountability would result in a loss of freedom. Little did I know that accountability enhances freedom. Obviously, his "off the wall" question made quite an imprint on me, else why would I recall the conversation after ten years?

Five years after this encounter a Roman Catholic priest and I were together in a support group. He identified another member of the group as his "spiritual director." Since seminary they had spent time together each month reporting on their life with God. One spring they had spent thirty days in the Sahara with the Little Brothers of Jesus. He witnessed to me about the value of spiritual direction. At the time I could not give myself to the idea; nevertheless, he reinforced the value of a spiritual director.

Not until two years ago did the matter of a spiritual director become a personal issue. I was consulting with a Christian organization in Chicago. The director made a statement that attracted my attention: "No person should give spiritual guidance to others unless he is receiving direction himself." That statement had my name on it. I continued to struggle with the challenge. My resistance to the thought of a director weakened. In fact, I felt a desire emerging within me for support, guidance, and accountability.

At the time of this new hunger I was experiencing significant changes in my life. For example, my interest in personal spiritual development was becoming an obsession with me. For months I had an insatiable appetite for reading spiritual literature. I found myself praying much more. I made several personal retreats. At the seminary I hosted three-day retreats to which eight or ten ministers came to find rest, encouragement, and silence. Most asked for guidance either from me or from the group.

I also began pondering new questions about a life

with God. Changes occurred in me that I did not understand. I felt a void because I had no one in my life with
whom to discuss them. God's approach to me took a
new form. Silence encroached on my prayers. I spoke
with God less and less. I listened more. Often I heard no
discernible words. I needed someone with whom to
discuss these new ways God was becoming manifest in
my life.

The future called for a deeper relationship with God,
yet I did not know how to achieve that depth. What
would it mean to be totally abandoned to the Spirit
of God?

This ferment in my life fueled my desire for a spiritual
director, a companion with whom I could talk over my
inner life. I did not need therapy. I did not feel malad-
justed or neurotic. I needed spiritual discernment, support, and guidance. Increasingly convinced that I
needed a spiritual director, I committed myself to
finding one. Little did I realize that my search would
extend over the better part of a year.

The Meaning of Spiritual Companion

The classical term "spiritual director" refers to one
who directs another in the spiritual life. Kenneth Leech
says, "The term 'spiritual direction' is usually applied to
the cure of souls when it involves the specific needs of
one individual."[1] Since the practice originated in the
Roman Catholic tradition, the idea of a priest guiding
one individual hints at "superior" priest, "inferior" lay
person, that is, authority/submission. This image
causes problems for Protestants.

To overcome this resistance, Urban Holmes has suggested several alternate names for the spiritual director.
He suggests "mystagogue," "one who leads us into
mystery."[2] The mystagogue, a mentor-type figure, leads
us into the mystery of our own being and into the deep
mystery of God.

Holmes said that the spiritual director may be like a

"hermeneut," a term derived from Greek mythology in which the god Hermes was a messenger between humans and the gods. The hermeneut calls into question cultural assumptions about the nature of the world, the activity of God, and our relation to God. The hermeneut communicates the message of God, not his or her own message, and is an instrument of knowing, a personal translator. The hermeneut travels the dangerous road between God and humans—the chaos, the dark, vast, confused and turbulent sea that lies between God and us—and enables us to face the demons and steer clear of the black holes. Holmes, like others, sees the immense need for spiritual guidance. He said, "We come to know ourselves, even our inner selves, as we reflect on the data of our experience with another."[3]

Other contemporary Protestant writers struggle with the term. While Holmes speaks of the "mystagogue" or the "hermeneut," Tilden Edwards calls this guide a "spiritual friend." Kenneth Leech speaks of a "soul friend." Another thinks of this person as a "faithful friend." I like the idea of a "spiritual companion."

The term "spiritual companion" suggests a fellow traveler, not a spectator; a seeker with me, not one who has arrived. A spiritual companion offers insight and information, not rules or regulations. This relationship holds me accountable to another out of free choice, not out of necessity. I follow the suggestions of my companion because of an earned respect, not because of a legalistic arrangement or an irrevocable vow.

This type of relationship originates in the New Testament itself. Models of spiritual companionship can be found in the Gospels, the Acts of the Apostles, and the epistles of Paul. Recall, for example, Jesus and the twelve. Peter, James, and John, in particular, found this guidance in their relationship with Jesus.

Paul was converted on his way to Damascus. On his arrival he began witnessing boldly to his faith in Jesus Christ. Yet when Paul came to Jerusalem, the apostles were suspicious of him. They were inclined to refuse him admission into their fellowship, but Barnabas vouched for him, declaring that Paul had seen the Lord and had witnessed vigorously for Christ in Damascus. Barnabas sponsored him in the faith and became his companion.

After the Jerusalem leadership commissioned Barnabas to establish a church in Antioch, he went to Tarsus to enlist the help of Paul, whom he took with him to Antioch. Together they taught there for a year. In those months Barnabas shared with Paul his love for, and knowledge of, Jesus Christ. After establishing this companionship, Barnabas and Paul became the first missionaries to the Gentiles.

The relationship of these two suggests a model for the development of a spiritual companionship. It began with a felt need Paul had for acceptance by the apostles. He also needed the instruction Barnabas offered. Barnabas's seeking out of Paul gave him a feeling of being needed for the ministry, a wise move on his mentor's part. In this companionship Paul had an opportunity to minister, to receive guidance, to have fellowship in prayer, and to experience the joy of preaching and the pain of rejection. The tension that arose between Paul and Barnabas suggests that spiritual companionships do not always progress smoothly. Conflict may arise even in the best intimate relation and cause it to be terminated. All these experiences are to be expected as we relate to a spiritual companion.

Searching for a Spiritual Companion

I asked God to lead me to the person who could offer the direction I needed. I sought God's guidance for this because I had not the slightest idea who that person would be.

Who were the persons in my life who could provide me with spiritual guidance? One by one I rejected the names on my roster. Some were too close; others were colleagues on the faculty, or persons about whom I felt some doubt. One person I desired was too busy; another, too far away. I considered the retreat master at the Monastery of the Holy Spirit. I also thought about going to a Jesuit priest. None of the options seemed right for me.

Assistance on this search came in a strange way. A minister friend came for an appointment on a subject far removed from spiritual direction. During our conversation, however, he mentioned John C. Smith (not his real name, of course). He described John's interest in the spiritual life and characterized him as a deeply spiritual man. My friend said, "I'd drive halfway across the country to spend one day with John." While he was describing this man, I exclaimed to myself, "That's it! He's the man!" Surely he would know that God had chosen him to give me spiritual direction. When I telephoned John for an appointment, I stated my need bluntly: "I want you to be my spiritual companion."

His immediate response was, "I'll be glad to meet with you and talk with you about your request." Since we did not know each other except by reputation, the conversation was quite brief. We made an appointment to meet in three weeks and said good-bye. As I heard the phone click in my ear, I realized that before meeting with him I had to think through my hopes and expectations from this relationship. I did not recognize how presumptuous I had been in assuming that he would be delighted to be a soul friend to me. I was sure he would ask me what I wanted from him, and I prepared an answer.

A Spiritual Companion: Character and Function

In the days that followed my telephone call with John, I began wondering what I would say to him. Had my impulsiveness gotten me into trouble? Would he be the right person for me? What qualities would I look for? I began reflecting on the essential characteristics for a spiritual companion.

First, I wanted someone who was spiritually mature—someone who had experienced a great deal of life and of God. I hoped for someone older than I, a wish probably influenced by the early death of my father. If I were to open my life to this person, I needed assurance that Christ was the center of his existence. He did not need to be perfect, but he would need to be absolutely serious about his relationship with God.

Second, I wanted someone who was knowledgeable in the ways of God, who knew the scriptures, the spiritual classics, and himself. My spiritual guide should unite his knowledge of himself with the best insights in human development because to be spiritual is to be fully human. Would John be this person?

My spiritual companion had to be an accepting person. Could John listen to the depths of my confession and still love me? I sought someone who would recognize my needs and accept me in spite of my immaturity and failures. The gift of acceptance provides the only atmosphere in which growth can occur.

I knew also that I needed honesty from my companion. Could he tell me honestly about himself? More important, could he be honest about his perceptions of me? I needed someone strong enough to confront me with my shallowness, my illusions, excuses, and rationalizations.

I wanted a guide I could trust implicitly. Trust does not immediately appear; it takes time and experience. But even in the first visit I would gather an impression about his trustworthiness. Does he seem interested in me? Am I comfortable with him? Will what I say be confidential? Can I count on him to walk through the tunnels of my life? These questions reached into the heart of a trusting relationship.

Finally, the person who would direct my journey must feel a call from God. Just as I had felt a call to search for a spiritual companion, he, too, must be called to accept this task. Responding yes too quickly might indi-

cate a lack of seriousness. Better that a person be too
hesitant than too eager.

Beginning the Relationship

At the appointed time I met with John and opened
the conversation by relating the way his name came to
me. I had never considered that he would be reluctant
to say yes to my request and so plunged ahead with talk
of my expectations. I was so sure God had guided me
to him that I thought he would be eager to begin the
task. Not so. How naive can a compulsive person be?

After hearing my request, he fumbled for excuses. He
did not know me personally, only by reputation. He did
not feel qualified. In short, he was reluctant to take
responsibility for guiding me. After pondering my request, he said candidly, "I can't offer you spiritual guidance."

"Why not?" I asked, taken aback.

"Because I am in such spiritual need myself that I
cannot give guidance to another."

With that confession, I waited. I could not press on
him another burden. I listened.

He continued, "I don't know anything about being a
spiritual director. I do know about direction from my
reading of the spiritual classics, and I have experienced
mutual counseling, but I have no experience with
spiritual direction. I don't know whether I can do that
or not."

Now it was my turn to speak. "I believe that God has
led me to you. I need you. I hope you will seriously
consider entering into this relationship with me."

"Only on one condition," he responded, "will I even
consider providing spiritual direction for you. I will do
it only if you will be a spiritual friend to me."

This response stunned me. In all my reflection on this
meeting I had not prepared myself for a request that I
guide him. Searching my own heart, I confessed, "I

don't feel competent to guide you. I need your help very much, but I don't think I'm mature enough to offer you any help."

"Well," he said, "only if you will become a spiritual companion to me will I offer the relationship to you."

Reluctantly I consented.

John continued, "I'm not agreeing today to accept this relationship, but I believe in providence enough to think that God may have sent you. You see, just a few days ago I asked God to help me with my prayer life. I have been negligent, undisciplined, and in great need of spiritual help. I have seemingly been incapable of disciplining myself to have regular times of prayer. I'm just enough of a Calvinist to believe that God may have sent you to me."

My need for help started with mutual spiritual direction as two confessed novices in need of God began a pilgrimage together. After finally agreeing to begin, we structured the experience by answering some basic questions. These suggestions may be helpful to you.

Be clear in your expectations. What do you want from your spiritual companion?

State your contract. Will this be a relationship of mutual spiritual direction? Mutual direction has limitations, but it is workable. When will you meet? For how long?

What are the goals of the relationship? Be sure that you understand the difference between fellowship and spiritual direction. While direction may include fellowship, it aims primarily at helping the individual relate to God. The director maintains control, guides the conversation, evaluates and responds to the experiences that are shared, and makes specific suggestions. This directive role separates spiritual direction from mutual sharing and fellowship.

If direction is to achieve its goals, it must be given priority. Conflicts will challenge every date. Placing this commitment before other responsibilities indicates the seriousness with which to take the quest for God.

Decide in the beginning how to structure the time together. Who will speak? Who will guide? How much time will be allotted to each? While the original structure can be changed as the relationship changes, an unambiguous structure saves time and minimizes confusion.

Decide before you begin the relationship how to terminate it. For example, you may wish to test the relationship for three months or six months, after which a new decision can be made. Both parties should understand that either person in the relationship can terminate the commitment if it is not working out.

From the beginning John and I had clearly stated objectives within an agreed on schedule. We met every two weeks and alternated in the role of director. The format began with a snack and a few minutes of small talk. We opened the session with silence; the directee broke the silence by offering prayer. Next, he brought his experiences of prayer and the struggles of his life to the attention of the director. The director responded, made suggestions, and shared his insights. Following this exchange, the issues were further discussed. The appointment was closed with prayer. Before departing, we checked the calendar for the next meeting. The encounter lasted from one and a half to two hours.

We followed this outline for a year. Our relationship took on increasing significance. Trust, respect, and acceptance grew. At the beginning of our second year we went to the Monastery of the Holy Spirit for a day's retreat. During that day our relationship reached a new depth. We discussed the tentativeness we had had in the beginning, the lack of commitment we both had, and the consequent barrier to the deepening of the relationship. We decided to set aside a day each month to spend in retreat at the monastery.

That decision called for a new structure of our time. Subsequently we would arrive at the monastery at about 9:30 in the morning, spend an hour in silence, and give the remainder of the morning to the director/directee relationship. Following the first encounter we would eat lunch, then rest briefly or take a silent walk.

In the afternoon we followed the morning schedule of silence, directing, and prayer, with the roles reversed. We found the prayer of the director for the directee at the close of the session to have immense value.

Problems in a Spiritual Companionship

A variety of problems may arise in the course of a spiritual companionship. For example, persons may simply be mismatched. You may have chosen a person who does not understand your journey and thus cannot be very helpful. Give yourself three or four months to test the relationship.

In the case of male/female spiritual companions, sexual attachments may develop. Face them openly and deal with them, or they will blur the direction and block spiritual progress.

Personality conflicts may occur. Many conflicts arise out of contradictory expectations. Other problems may appear when the relationship needs to be terminated, because the director has helped as much as he or she can or because of some other reason. (Be careful not to use this situation as an excuse for avoiding barriers.) Persons who refuse to obey the leading of the Spirit will find numerous ways to avoid dealing with problems and conflicts; but until barriers are faced, growth will cease. Getting through these resistances calls forth the skill and perseverance of the director.

Whatever the problem, it must be dealt with. A good process begins with acknowledging the problem and naming it. Second, identify your options for dealing with that problem. Make your choice and follow the plan you design. If problems cannot be resolved, the relationship may have to be terminated, as provided for in the contract. However, the ending of a relationship need not rupture the friendship.

Values of a Spiritual Companionship

When John and I began meeting together regularly, I did not know what to expect. During nearly two years of sharing our spiritual life together, I made some insightful discoveries.

I have been helped immeasurably by being accountable to another person. I have been accountable for our meeting together, stating my progress on the spiritual journey, confessing my struggles, and facing the decisions I need to make. Voluntarily making myself accountable to John on these issues has given me great freedom.

Once John said to me, "I don't know why I'm more accountable to you than I am to God. If I promise you that I will do a particular thing, I usually do it. But I find it so easy to go back on my promises to God." Why is it harder to face a person to whom you have broken a promise than to face God?

Such is the importance of accountability!

I have discovered greater clarity through articulating my experiences to another person. Experiences that occur at the edge of silence come as an undifferentiated mass of feelings, inspirations, and intuitions. Not until I can put these into words do the experiences become understandable to me.

I have received insight from my spiritual companion. He has provided guidance from his experiences, from his knowledge of the classics, and from his sensitivity to the Spirit's work in my life. He has shown me the firm theological foundation Calvin laid for the spiritual life and repeatedly affirms, "Accept all of life as from God!"

I have discovered personal support for my journey. Not only have I been accepted, affirmed, appreciated, and given words of assurance about God's work in my life, but I have known the incalculable support of prayer from a man who knows me and who cares about God's work in my life. I no longer feel alone in my struggle.

On one occasion I shared with my spiritual companion the struggle I have with overeating. I confessed, "I need help in getting a grip on my compulsive eating; I feel threatened sometimes by the power food has over me."

He studied my confession for a few moments, then asked, "Have you ever fasted?"

"Yes."

"I recommend that you fast one day each week and look to God rather than to food."

When I agreed to his suggestion, he added this statement: "I will join you in the fast, and I will pray for you every day that we fast together."

Can you imagine the support that a struggling person feels when someone cares enough to identify with his failure, frustration, and guilt? To give me strength and encouragement, a man who did not need to lose weight or control his appetite joined me in my struggle. I felt the power of his self-sacrifice on my behalf.

My spiritual companion has served as a marker. Like a channel marker in the river that guides unwary travelers, he has steered me away from the rocks and kept me from plunging over the dam. His perception of me and of my unique journey with God has offered an objectivity I could gain no other way. Each meeting has enabled me to adjust, focus, and reaffirm my intent to follow the will of God. These gifts are of inestimable worth to me and cause me to search more diligently for God's purpose in my life.

A Postscript to Spiritual Companionship

Out of my experience I offer the following suggestions for finding a spiritual companion.

If you engage a spiritual companion, keep it a secret. Nothing is quite so out of place as making public your intimate dealings with your soul. Exposing the details of this sacred relationship would be distasteful and ill advised, to say nothing of breaking a trust based on confidentiality.

Keep your relationship one of spiritual companionship, not of friendship or socializing. You are meeting with a spiritual companion to "help each other on to God." Nothing else should interfere.

Always pray with and for your companion.

Be patient with your growth. Do not expect to make great spiritual advances at every meeting. Some days may involve nothing more than checking in with each other in the presence of God.

Learn to appreciate the small advances, both in yourself and in your companion. In the short view we do not know what the growth is. We must be faithful and count on God to bring about the changes God wills for us.

Keep a journal. Reflect on your entries in the journal as preparation for meeting your spiritual companion.

Knowing how reluctant I was for years to make myself accountable to a spiritual companion, I understand the hesitation of anyone considering this step. But my experience with this particular path to spiritual growth allows me to commend it as a valuable way of regulating your life with God.

Use the exercise for chapter 5 in Appendix A to help you sort out your feelings and make some decisions about spiritual companionship.

6

Journey in the Kingdom Vision

*The vision within
must be made concrete in history.*

Journeying to the center must be balanced with a kingdom vision to connect you with the concrete events of your history. This vision of the future will constantly remind you of the goal, not only for yourself but for all persons. The kingdom vision will prevent your getting lost in the inner world of subjective experiences. "Thy kingdom come; thy will be done on earth as it is in heaven" unites the inner world of silence with the external world of action; it also points to the power that translates vision into historical reality.

As you have explored a number of pathways on your journey into the Mystery, you have seen that the central prayer for this movement with God is "Thy will be done." This request reaches beyond the personal to the corporate; it impacts history. So this profound spiritual journey that you have undertaken has direct social implications.

The preceding phrase in the Lord's Prayer suggests as much: "Thy kingdom come." Consider the profound implications of those three simple words.

"Thy kingdom come" means:

For all persons to acknowledge that they are children of God
For all to reverence God

For all to do God's will on earth as it is done in heaven

When all persons are God's children, and reverence God's name, and do God's will on earth as it is done in heaven:

All will have their daily bread.
All will forgive and be forgiven their debts.
All will be led by God's hand.
All will be delivered from darkness.

When this transformation comes to pass, the kingdom of this world will have become the kingdom of our God and of the Lord Christ. And he shall reign for ever and ever!

The prayer we pray leads to the kingdom for which the world waits, a kingdom of justice, of peace, of righteousness, and the fear of the Lord.

The kingdom lies in the future. As pilgrims we live with a vision of a new heaven and a new earth. With our hearts purified and our visions refined, we live with a hope of what may become, through the generous love of God, the kingdom of God being made actual among us on earth. An inventor in a science fiction story devised a "timescope," a telescope that could look through time, and discovered that having a vision of the future dramatically changed his perception of the present. In the same way for us, once we get a glimpse of the new heaven and the new earth, everything we do in the present will be influenced by that vision.

The kingdom vision exists today in the heart of a woman who struggles to rear her children alone, but it is not actualized completely in her; it manifests itself in the life of a worker who strives for an adequate wage to care for his family; the vision appears in the soul of an industrialist who institutes safety measures and profit sharing, but even this generosity and compassion leave the full realization of the kingdom in a distant future.

Journeying to the center will require a kingdom vision
to connect you with the concrete events of history. This
vision of the future will constantly remind you of life's
goal, not only for yourself but for all persons. It will
prevent your getting lost in the inner world of subjective
experiences. "Thy kingdom come; thy will be done on
earth as it is in heaven" unites the inner world of silence
with the external world of action; it points to the power
that translates vision into historical reality.

My spiritual companion and I were returning from the
monastery after a day's retreat when I asked him,
"What does it mean to you to be a kingdom person?"

"I've never heard it put just like that," he responded.
Then this near saint of a man began to reflect on his
vision of the kingdom. "I guess," he began, "that I have
always thought of the kingdom of God as God's rule,
God's will done on earth as it is in heaven.

"My first vision of the kingdom of God came through
E. Stanley Jones. He wrote a number of devotional
books in which he spelled out the meaning of peace,
justice, and equality for all of God's people.

"As you know, he was deeply influenced by Walter
Rauschenbusch, the great social gospeler of the early
twentieth century. Jones, though, had the unique gift of
uniting his social passion with a deep piety. Whatever
I know about the kingdom has surely been influenced
by these two giant souls."

He paused reflectively. "I have endeavored through
the years to hold two great forces in tension: a genuine
devotion to God and a life of servanthood in the world.
In a profound way the life of a kingdom person must
be grounded in a deeply personal relationship with God.
Of course, this devotion expresses itself in our natural
callings—being a friend, a devoted husband, a reliable
father, an honest worker. But with Jones and Rauschenbusch I believe this devotion must be expressed
socially in the pressing issues of the day."

"As you look back on your life, what effect has this
vision had on the way you live your life?" I asked.

He mused for a few minutes before he spoke. A flood of memories seemed to rise to the surface of his mind. Then he spoke. "I suppose the first way this vision influenced my life centered on the issue of race. I could not reconcile the kingdom of God as it is described in the Bible with the practice of segregation. Early on, I had to take a stand, and that meant paying a price.

"Then," he continued, "I have been a pacifist. I cannot see that taking another person's life in military combat will ever fulfill the will of God. Violence begets violence! Of course, by rejecting war as a means to peace, I have to resist the use of all nuclear arms—in fact, the whole military buildup in which our country is engaged.

"This perspective is like a garment that begins to unravel with the pulling of just one thread. When you disagree, as I do, with your nation's stand on war, paying taxes becomes a matter of conscience. I must confess that I have not avoided paying my due tax, but I have taken a salary cut so that what tax I pay is modest. I also send a letter saying that I do not wish my payment spent on the war machine."

I found his candor and forthright witness to the kingdom an inspiration, so I asked him, "In what other ways today is your vision of the kingdom affecting your life?"

He continued, "I have never felt that great wealth was an aid to one's spirituality. John Woolman says, 'I have noticed that the increase of wealth is usually accompanied by the increase of the desire for more.' I have tried to live simply. I do not need many material goods; what I have is sufficient, and I have no desire to be a wealthy man.

"If we are kingdom people, we live in the vision of how God has remade the world in Christ. We do not see peace. We do not see equality. But we live with a vision of peace, justice, and equality. Everything in this world that contradicts this vision, we must be against; and everything that will propel this vision forward, we must give our energies to support."

What a vision! What a commitment of life! I asked, "In light of this faith, are you an optimist or a pessimist?"

"If I were dependent on human effort to bring in the kingdom, I would be a consummate pessimist. We will not bring in the kingdom, though we work for it with all our might.

"I am an optimist because I believe that the kingdom is a gift of God. God will give the kingdom when and as God wills."

As I reflected on this conversation, the one thing that impacted me most strongly was the awareness that this friend really lived every day what he had shared with me. I know him. I know his soul, and he is this kind of person living with a vision of the kingdom of God.

I think that he is as near a saint as my denomination has produced. He has been to the center. He has listened to the Spirit. He has returned with face aglow and heart aflame to make actual in our time what he beheld in the face of God. This testimony points toward the kind of person who lives with a kingdom vision.

All persons live by the dictates of a vision. They absorb their original picture of reality from their community of origin, and it directs their lives until they examine it and consciously adopt an alternative. The prevailing vision of modern persons has a certain dullness when it comes to a God-awareness in the events of the day. One goal of the spiritual journey has been to subvert the common picture of reality and to offer direction toward the new earth vision. This final task calls us to explore the way from the kingdom within to the concrete manifestation of the kingdom in history and beyond.

The Kingdom Within

Jesus said, "The kingdom of God is not coming with signs to be observed . . . for behold, the kingdom of God is in the midst of you" (Luke 17:20–21). The spiritual journey begins with the fact that we are; we have come into this world of being; we are and we know that we are. Each of us decides on a structure for our time and on the narrative we tell about the events and encounters along the way. These are the primal realities of every journey.

Buried deep within each heart is the cry for meaning, a yearning satisfied by shaping the events of our lives into a story. Each of our stories has a beginning and an end. The narrative we tell of the events occurring between these two points expresses our life's meaning.

To find the ultimate meaning of your life, you must connect your personal story with the larger story of history, God's story. This connection requires a knowledge of the traditional symbols of the faith and their power to open your life to its deeper meaning.

The initial entry into the world of the Spirit and the expansion of your awareness of God in your life comes through God's initiative and a response of personal prayer. In this disciplined experience you intentionally open yourself to God.

This exposing of your consciousness to God in private finds a deeper grounding in the liturgy of a worshiping community. Structured prayer offers you individually what the liturgy gives to the corporate community.

You can discover your own whole life experience in the Divine Presence. Through the confession of your life, you can find a new depth of forgiveness, acceptance, and healing. God's acceptance will put to rest some of the inner noises of your life, permitting you to hear the voice of God through the silence.

Meditation opens the way to a new depth of the knowledge of God. By focusing your mind on God's truth, you will find ways to permit the Word of God to sink into your soul.

Contemplation takes you beyond the rational search for truth by opening the unconscious depths of the psyche. This receptive opening to your depths enables you to receive the images and impulses that arise below consciousness. Through the media of dreams, twilight imaging, and openness to the events of your life, you begin to discern the movement of God in your life.

God comes to you through the events of your life. By listening to the data of experience, the occurrences that impact your consciousness daily, you are able to listen, to discern the meaning of your unfolding life.

The desert, the deep world of silence, takes you from the external world of noise and distraction to listen to the still small voice within. Silence opens the door and leads you to the center point, the border of the kingdom within, where you see the connecting point to all things.

As you near the center, you have only begun to approach the kingdom's expression in the social order. The kingdom journey is a long one. "The longest journey is the journey inwards," said Dag Hammarskjöld. Longest because it is deepest. Because it is farther. Because it takes more time.

After entering the desert and wrestling with your demons and discovering your angels, you come to "the still point"—a place of peace, a point at which you begin to feel at home with yourself and with life. At the center you discover a fountain of grace that offers you a reconciled relationship with God, with yourself, with others, and with life itself. At the center point, do not expect too much or settle for too little. Accept life, the real life in the world, in God. At the center point you will be infused with courage to become what you were created to be!

The center is not only our center but the center of all things. It is the source of being; it is like an umbilical cord that was once connected to the Creator. Though this center is within us, we do not have control over it. We cannot approach it in our own power; we cannot attach ourselves to it. We are drawn toward it and occasionally given a taste of unity with it.

A fragile membrane on the underside of this center point separates being and not being. From this center point gushes energy. The power of being springs forth from this depth, a power that not only calls us into being but sustains every created thing. But do not confuse this center with yourself. The center is within us, yet it always infinitely transcends us. All things that exist find their source in this center. And at this center "everything is connected with everything."

The connectedness of all things at the center means that all creation emerges from and converges at this point. This center unifies all the diverse aspects of being. At the center a tree finds its connection with a stone; the molecules of matter find their union with spirit; the loftiest dreams of the human heart find their union with the Divine Spirit. Everything connects to everything! And the vision of this unity is a gift. It is the kingdom of God!

The center contains "the beginning of the road to everywhere"! For at the center, we encounter the God of creation and the Lord of history. There we listen to the personal Christ who is our personal savior, as well as the cosmic Christ who is Lord of the universe. He who rules the universe is the source of our being, the Lord of our life, and the goal of history!

The Kingdom Without

The kingdom within, which arises through the center point of being, encounters an opposing kingdom without. The kingdom of Light wars against the kingdom of Darkness. In the kingdom of Darkness powers clash, evil reigns, destruction wipes out life. The world of Darkness resists the kingdom of Light. To manifest itself in a world dominated by sin, the kingdom of Light must war against evil, darkness, and death. Our lives are caught in the battle between these two cosmic forces.

The kingdom of Darkness is characterized by alienation, conflict, oppression, idolatry, and ignorance. You are not a stranger to this kingdom. The power of destruction affects all our lives. Alienation means separation—separation from God, from oneself, from others, and from a sense of belonging in the world. Even nature wears the face of an enemy when her storms blow us off course and her earthquakes swallow thousands of lives.

In our personal journey to the center of our being we have cried out for our identity, a cry we make for a very long time. The alienation from ourself, manifest in our constant search for identity, characterizes the whole world. The little boy feels separated from his parents and longs for the security of belonging. The computer programmer sitting at her keyboard feels alienated from the warmth of persons. The scientist isolated in a laboratory feels estranged from the rest of the world. This "not-at-homeness" results from life being broken apart—the kingdom of Darkness.

The kingdom of Darkness is further characterized by conflict, a war between good and evil. On our journey we have discovered our own darkness and in this darkness met our own contradictions. For example, the good intention to pray with greater discipline always meets resistance. Even more serious, the journey inward opens despised parts of ourself. None of us is pure. The evil imaginations that have possessed us, the hidden sins that no one else knows, and the lustful dreams for power and recognition appear so shameful in the light of a suffering God of love.

Anger with our failure or resistance to some part of our life issues in an internal war. This war within us finds a counterpart in our struggle with the people in our lives. Our personal failings are projected onto others, the corporate conflicts of groups or persons are projected on the nation, and nations that make war project their fear on one another.

The kingdom of Darkness is characterized by oppression, the use of power to gain advantage over another. All oppression—economic, political, social, and sexual—stems from greed. Power makes possible the fulfillment of greed. No matter how much we possess, we are like the man in Jesus' parable who wanted to pull down his barns and build larger ones (Luke 12:18). The urge to have more and more plagues our souls. Compound the greed of individuals with that of corporations and you have a major source of an oppressive society. In their greed, corporations with an almost limitless power to oppress grind up their own employees with high demands, lobby and obtain favorable legislation, and organize their goals for the sake of the bottom line. A consumer nation like our own is the composite of individual and corporate greed. How powerful is the kingdom of Darkness! How often it prevails!

Ignorance reigns in the kingdom of Darkness. In those areas of life void of the knowledge of the truth, or of God, darkness prevails. This darkness shows its underside as superstition and fear. The journey to truth in the natural world traverses a large sea of ignorance. Where ignorance of the truth reigns, the kingdom of Darkness prevails.

Where the true God is not known, persons turn to substitute gods, to idols. Devotion to the gods of success, pleasure, intellectualism, politics—even religion, good though it is—is nevertheless idolatry. A young man graduates from the university full of vision for his future. He gives himself to his job, imagining that it will fulfill the cry of his soul for meaning. It does, briefly. But once he has achieved his goal, the old haunting cry returns. The idol of success does not satisfy permanently.

Finally, death reigns in the kingdom of Darkness. The kingdom of Darkness has no power of being within itself; it lives off the kingdom of Light. All that participates in it will ultimately perish; evil will be swept along in the tide of death. The destructive consequences of the dark rule on this earth will one day be obliterated; its negative creations will eventually be lost to the memory of God.

Each of us understands all too well the kingdom of Darkness. It is part of us. Each participates in its alienation, conflict, idolatry, ignorance, and death.

The kingdom of Darkness does not reign uninhibited. It encounters the kingdom of Light. The kingdom of Light shows its passion in salvation, reconciliation, justice, compassion, and the knowledge of God. Our individual journeys take us through time in the midst of these conflicting forces. The data of our lives include elements of both; yet our choices tend either to support one kingdom or the other.

The kingdom of Light has the character of salvation. Salvation means the healing of estrangement in persons and in groups. Salvation unites persons with God and with themselves. Nouwen tells of three old men, one of whom had a very bad reputation, who came to Abba Achilles. The first two asked the Abba to make them a fishnet. He refused, saying that he was too busy. The third, the one with the bad reputation, also asked him to make a fishnet. The Abba immediately said yes.

The others asked, "Why did you make the third man a fishnet and not one for us?" The old Abba responded, "If I had not made him a net, he would have said, 'The old man has heard about my sin, and that is why he does not want to make me anything.' And so our relationship would have broken down. Now I have cheered his soul so that he will not be overcome with grief."[1] The kingdom of Light shines on all, especially those who are oppressed by the weight of their own sin.

The kingdom of Light is a kingdom of reconciliation. The Light also seeks the resolution of conflict between persons and groups. It heals families, races, sexes, and nations of their tensions. Wherever we discern reconciliation taking place, there is the kingdom of Light.

When a father reaches out to an estranged son offering love even though he knows it will be rejected, that promises reconciliation. When a few persons raise a cry against their own government for its support of repressive military forces, their agony has the feeling of reconciliation. When a pastor opens her congregation's eyes to the needs of the homeless, she models reconciliation.

The kingdom of Light seeks justice for all. Justice translates love into freedom for the oppressed and justice for the powerless. Because it is a kingdom of justice, it is filled with hope and the possibility for jobs, education, and leadership without discrimination. If everything is connected to everything, no citizen of the light can rest easy until all the peoples of the world have equality and justice.

An illustration of what I mean is found in Alan Paton's novel, *Ah, But Your Land Is Beautiful,* which depicts the recent struggles in South Africa.

Robert Mansfield, a white South African, resigns as headmaster of a white school because its football team is not allowed to play a black school's team. More basically, he resigns because, as he says, "I think it is time to go out and fight everything that separates people from one another."

Mansfield is visited by Emmanuel Nene, a black. He wants to see what a white man who would do such a thing looks like. He, a black, is about to join a multiracial political group, a step that will also brand him as an enemy of the state. In the narrative Mansfield welcomes Nene and warns him of the possibility of harm.

Nene replies, "Yes . . . I'm going to get wounded also. Not only by the Government, but by my own people as well. . . . Some of them will say, Why don't you stay with your own people? . . . Why get mixed up with these white people, who are rich while you are poor?"

The story continues:

> Mr. Nene rose, and looked cheerfully around him.
> "I don't worry about the wounds. When I go up there,

which is my intention, the Big Judge will say to me,
Where are your wounds? and if I say I haven't any, he will
say, Was there nothing to fight for?"

Emmanuel leaves. And, Paton concludes, Mansfield—left alone—"felt a burst of hope for the future. . . . He had in fact had an encounter with the
light."[2]
The kingdom of Light is a kingdom of compassion
where mercy sets the tone of all relationships. Henri
Nouwen says, "To die to our neighbors means to stop
judging them, to stop evaluating them, and thus to become free to become compassionate. Compassion can
never coexist with judgment because judgment creates
the distance, the distinction, which prevents us from
really being with the other."[3] Compassion conquers violence.
After years of struggle Carretto hammered out his
confession of the kingdom of Light. "When I first
became active in the Church and was going through
my paces," he says, "I did not know the distinction between a defensive war and a holy war. Today,
now that I am close to death, I no longer believe in
either.

I believe in nonviolence.
I believe in the blood of the innocent.
I believe in winning by losing.
I believe in true disarmament.
I believe in the wolf of Gubbio.
I believe in the potential of a people who no longer
take up arms even when surrounded by armed peo-
ples.
I believe in prophecy more than in politics.
I believe in Gandhi.
I believe in Martin Luther King.
I believe in Archbishop Romero.
I believe in Pope John Paul, who after two assassi-
nation attempts continues to go unarmed among the
crowds with his hand raised in greeting.[4]

Carretto believes and hopes in the kingdom of God!

Another feature characterizes this kingdom. The kingdom of Light is a kingdom of the knowledge of God. Habakkuk said that "the earth will be filled with the knowledge of the glory of the LORD, as the waters cover the sea" (Hab. 2:14). Jeremiah exclaimed that we shall no longer say, " 'Know the LORD,' for they shall all know [him], from the least of them to the greatest" (Jer. 31:34).

None of us can soon forget Martin Luther King, Jr.'s final address. In it he expressed some concern about his life and the length of it. He allowed that God had already let him ascend the mountain and look over into the Promised Land.

The next day he was assassinated.

How do we recognize the kingdom of Light amid the kingdom of Darkness? What are the signs or structures of the kingdom? Though the kingdom manifests itself through structures, we should never confuse the structures with the kingdom itself. Rather, the concrete expressions of justice, compassion, reconciliation, and salvation in history point to the reality of the kingdom of God. To lift specific acts of mercy and compassion to kingdom status fails to recognize the ambiguous nature of every act of love. Every manifestation of the kingdom of Light possesses an element of the Darkness. The kingdom is breaking in but will not manifest itself in any particular political, social, or economic form until the kingdom comes and God's will is done on earth as it is in heaven.

If the kingdom is in our midst, if indeed it is breaking into the world through the structures of history, how does the kingdom of Light interact with the kingdom of Darkness? What is their relationship in our common history?

The kingdom of Light functions throughout the universe; it is not a phenomenon limited to the western world. The Spirit of God actualizes the kingdom in every nation, in a variety of cultural forms, and through nearly all religious traditions. This kingdom must be known by its structures of justice, compassion, salvation, and healing. The God of history seeks through persons like you and me to actualize the kingdom incarnationally in every historical tradition.

The kingdom aims to conquer the power of darkness, to resist evil, and to actualize the will of God in concrete embodiments in history. Wherever that embodiment occurs, the kingdom of God is manifesting itself.

The kingdom of Light in history always appears paradoxical in nature, which means that the kingdom both is and is not manifest. For example, Jesus asserted in the Gospels that the kingdom of God "is not of this world." It does not arise out of this world's planning, scheming, and desiring. The kingdom always comes as a gift from God. But persons choose the kingdom and function in a way that aspects of the kingdom become visible and tangible. The manifestation of the kingdom both is and is not a human achievement. The kingdom always concerns itself with events in this world even though it does not originate here (John 17:15; 18:36).

The kingdom of God is a gift, but it does not come cheaply. Jesus said, "Fear not, little flock; for it is your Father's good pleasure to give you the kingdom" (Luke 12:32). Yet those who receive the kingdom as a gift are called to sacrifice everything for it.

The kingdom is not mere talk (1 Cor. 4:20), but it must be proclaimed (Luke 4:43). Jesus proclaimed the kingdom of God not only in the words he spoke but in his whole life. To paraphrase Charles de Foucauld, "Jesus shouted the gospel from the rooftop, not so much by what he said but by how he lived." "The kingdom of God does not mean food and drink," says Paul (Rom. 14:17). But the coming of the kingdom has been compared to a wedding feast (Matt. 22:1–14).

The kingdom is invisible. It "is not coming with signs to be observed" (Luke 17:20). But it is evident to those who can discern its presence. And on the last day "every eye will see him" (Rev. 1:7).

Because of its paradoxical nature the kingdom is always a mixture. It is already here, but we pray for it to come. The kingdom is a field of wheat that is mixed with the tares. It is a net cast into the sea, which is filled with good fish and bad. And so it will be until the climax of history when the paradox will vanish in the fulfillment of the purpose of God.

The kingdom of God is within us, but it stretches beyond us. We participate in it, but it transcends us infinitely; it existed before us and will be after us. But in the moment of our personal histories, we participate in the actualization of the kingdom vision. The struggle takes a personal form within each of us. As we struggle within ourselves, this wrestling mirrors the cosmic struggle going on outside of us. Our inward journey leads us to self-conscious participation in the larger unfolding drama of history.

Each life journey constitutes but a paragraph in the story of God. Yet contemplation of our unique life journey unites us with ourself and the meaning of our one and only life; it also enables us to participate in the larger purpose of God for our life and for human history. To grasp the chapters of our lives offers greater self-understanding, but this awareness in the context of the purpose of God infuses life with ultimate meaning. Our personal lives are united with the Creator of all things, and our individual stories form a portion of the fulfillment of the eternal purpose of God. These concrete chapters of our lives manifest a portion of the kingdom of Light, a light that shines in the darkness and the darkness cannot conquer it.

The examination of our consciousness through reflecting on a day of our life opens the meaning of a small segment of history. In this capsule of the kingdom, we recognize trends, movements, and directions for our existence. As we intentionally direct the movement of our lives toward kingdom ends, we become kingdom people manifesting the will and power of God in the world.

Through meditation we draw on the image of Christ to discern our own depths. Out of those depths fresh images fill our mind with the content of the kingdom in our time and place. The image of Christ provides the norm for kingdom living; it enables us to discern the movement of the Spirit in our life and in the world.

Worship constantly restructures our time through Jesus Christ. In each service of worship we recall that all before him was preparation and all that comes after is fulfillment of God's purpose. Before the ultimate fulfillment of all things in Christ we encounter him through the Word. In the sacrament we recall his death for our sins, but as we break the bread and drink the wine, we anticipate his final triumph. So worship structures time as past, present, and future, a then, a now, and a when!

All movement in history has meaning for God, both the internal movement of the searching soul and the external movement of events. Each movement occurs through God's providence and has the potential for fulfilling God's purpose and person. The meaning created by our life will never be lost but will be preserved in the memory of God forever. Heaven must surely include the reliving of our stories and the discovery of where they fit in the cosmic scheme of things.

Use the exercises for chapter 6 in Appendix A to help you sustain your vision of the kingdom.

A New Earth Vision

John said, "Then I saw a new heaven and a new earth; for the first heaven and the first earth had passed away" (Rev. 21:1). How does the inner reality relate to the outer reality? Is it an ideal? What role does the kingdom vision fill? Where does the vision originate, and how does it grasp us?

Just what is this vision of a new heaven and a new earth? What will it be? The new earth vision is a vision

of fulfilled humanity: the fulfillment of persons, relationships, systems, and nations. These are fulfilled only by
subjecting themselves to the intention of God and the
ultimate aim God has for them. The new earth must be
one of reconciliation, compassion, mercy, justice, and
equality.

The new earth vision means a vision of God, a deep,
profound encounter with the Holy One. It means a cen-
tering of life where God is all.

The new earth vision is a projection of the union of
the inner and the outer worlds. It is a symbol of the
actualization of what we have encountered in the depth
of our being; namely, a vision of the Mystery, the Origin
of us all.

Where does this vision come from? How does it originate? It does not come by human efforts through either
meditation or contemplation. It does not come through
the effort of confession, purification, or worship.

The new earth vision comes as a gift. It originates
through an encounter with the Spirit; it expresses itself
as a symbol that enables us to perceive it. We cannot
hold on to it. The vision has a life and purpose of its
own. It tends to come and go of its own accord. The
vision of a new heaven and a new earth may come
suddenly or gradually; however, it grasps us firmly and
guides the direction of our lives. Most often we do not
seek the vision; the vision seeks us.

A lonely man in an ancient country hears the voice
saying, "I will make of you a great nation." Though
realizing the fulfillment of the promise was far off, he
still obeyed the call.

The prophet did not hear God in the wind or in the
earthquake, but in "the still small voice."

On the mountaintop three frightened disciples of
Jesus hear a voice in the cloud saying, "This is my own
dear Son. Listen to him."

Two men walk along a dusty road talking about their
dashed hopes and shattered dreams. A stranger appears and walks with them. He speaks of history, recent

happenings, and those with whom he journeyed. He accepts their hospitality, enters their house, and breaks bread. And the breaking of the bread opens their eyes to who he is. Revelation reaches beyond rationality. They understand why their hearts burned within them as he talked with them on the road.

In an upper room a crowd waits in prayer. Suddenly, the Divine breaks through with signs of fire and wind. They hear emphatically, "Go and teach all nations."

A group of dedicated disciples wait, fast, and pray. The Spirit of God speaks, "Separate unto me Barnabas and Saul for the work to which I have called them." A vision for the mission of Christ possesses them.

To what end is this vision of a new heaven and a new earth? Why does it come to us? Why does it grasp us? The new earth vision comes to us as a guide, takes us by the hand, and leads us through the darkness, assuring us of the way. The vision keeps hope alive. It steers us in the right direction. It is an ideal, but more than an ideal. It is the future coming to meet us, and the vision signifies its arrival.

The new earth vision inspires courage. When the actuality seems so far away, it beckons us to go on. The vision inspires sacrifice, even to dying like a Bonhoeffer or a Polycarp. These men had "seen" something.

The vision given to us keeps faith alive when the power of darkness seems to prevail.

Yes, the new earth vision will prevail.

Isaiah saw the vision and was possessed by it. He wrote:

Have you not known? Have you not heard?
The LORD is the everlasting God,
    The Creator of the ends of the earth.
He does not faint or grow weary,
    his understanding is unsearchable.
He gives power to the faint,
    and to him who has no might he increases strength.
Even youths shall faint and be weary
    and young men shall fall exhausted;

but they who wait for the LORD shall renew their strength,
  they shall mount up with wings like eagles,
they shall run and not be weary,
  they shall walk and not faint.

(Isaiah 40:28–31)

Between the promise of God, the vision of the kingdom, and the actualization of that kingdom, there is much to do. We are called to be kingdom persons, to actualize the compassion, forgiveness, reconciliation, and justice of the kingdom in our free choices, and that is often more of a challenge than most of us desire.

My friend of many years told me about his experience with the kingdom vision. Now retired, he had given a month of his time to live at Koinonia Farms, a self-supporting religious community in Americus, Georgia. He had helped with the mailings, packing foodstuffs for sale, and had generally served the needs of the community.

The day of his departure had come. He was packed, ready to leave. But having heard that Ladon Sheats had come in the night before, he decided to go by and see him. Ladon had spent more time in jail the last five years than he had spent free. His incarceration had been for his protests of nuclear proliferation.

Considering the pain and mistreatment Ladon had been through, my friend expected him to be hard, perhaps bitter. No matter, he stopped by the house to say hello and good-bye.

When Ladon came to the door, he looked into the face of my friend, smiled, and said softly, "Come in; glad to see you."

My friend and his wife entered. They spoke for a few minutes. Their visit ended, they prepared to leave. Ladon urged him to stay and share the stories of their lives the last few years.

"I can't," my friend said. "We have to be going on. Hope to see you another time."

As he was reliving the story, my friend turned to me

and said, "I've never seen a man at greater peace. He is warm, cheerful, and caring. He shows no scars from his witness.

"You know, I could have stayed and listened to his story, but I didn't want to. I didn't want to know the pain he had suffered. I didn't want to feel the weight of God's conviction in my own heart. So I said, 'I have to go.'"

As we open ourselves to the vision of God, let us never underestimate the power of sin, the grip of selfishness, the desire not to know so that we may escape the conviction of the God who has called us not only to see a vision of the kingdom but to live a kingdom life.

The kingdom comes in the concrete events of our existence. God will come to dwell in our midst. When the kingdom comes, there will be no more separation, no more alienation. God will be with us and we will be with God. We will be God's people forever. Between now and then there are many risks to take!

The journey began a long time ago in the mind of God. At our appointed time we entered the stream to live out our obedience to God and thus make our contribution to the story. Soon our time will be ended, and we will enter the lasting memory of God.

May we in the time appointed us live as people with a vision!

Appendixes

Appendix A

Exercises

Reading about the spiritual journey has little practical value. New ideas are of value only when we reflect on our life with God. One aid to the process of reflection is a personal spiritual journal.

The journal may be any type of record from a spiral notebook to a computer. The journal contains your insights and spiritual discoveries. It is both personal and private.

These exercises offer guidance in the types of entries to make in your journal. The exercises may also be used with classes or groups.

Exercise for Chapter 1
Meditation on the Journey

Spend several days meditating on the significant events in the life of Jesus:

The announcement of his birth (Luke 1:26–38)
The birth of Jesus (Luke 2:1–20)
The baptism of Jesus (Matt. 3:13–17)
The first sermon of Jesus (Luke 4:16–21)
The transfiguration of Jesus (Mark 9:2–13)

The upper room experience (John 13)
The garden prayer (Matt. 26:36–46)
The death of Jesus (Matt. 27:45–56)
The resurrection of Jesus (John 20:11–18)
The ascension of Jesus (Acts 1:6–11)

In your meditation on the life of Jesus, ask the following questions:

1. What happened? What are the facts?
2. In what context did this experience occur?
3. What did the writer want the original reader to know?
4. What did this experience mean in the life of Jesus? How can I connect my life experience with his?
5. What will I do because of these insights? What new decisions will I make about my life?

Take whatever time you need to work your way through these events in the life of Jesus. Let yourself feel the movement of the Spirit in the life of Jesus. At the same time you are letting the mind of Christ form within you.

Reflect on the writings of Paul for an understanding of the meaning of Christ's life, death, and resurrection:

Romans 1–8
1 Corinthians 13
Ephesians 1:15–23 and 3:14–21
Galatians 2:20

Exercise for Chapter 2
Journey Into the Contemplation of God

This chapter describes a way to contemplate Christ through the scriptures. The following suggestions offer a step-by-step guide. The passages from the Gospel of Mark will provide a variety of healings with which you can identify.

Suggestions for Getting Into the Scriptures

1. Select a passage from the following section, "The Healings of Jesus," which seems to speak directly to you.

2. Read the passage reflectively.

3. Identify the person in the passage most like you.

4. Enter into the situation through the person with whom you identify. (To enter the situation, relax. Close your eyes. Picture the person with whom you identify. View the whole situation through this person's eyes.)

5. Write your perceptions in your journal. Write in the first person: "I." Be sure to write all the perceptions that come to you. Include situation, place, feelings, reactions, images, and requests. Let your imagination be free to explore tangents to the narrative. Let it take you where it will.

6. After writing a description of the events you have seen, felt, heard, engage Jesus in a dialogue. Ask him a question that comes to you naturally. Then write his response. Keep up the dialogue until you "feel finished."

7. After writing, sit quietly. Be with the experience. Reexperience the wholeness of this encounter. Be with the experience.

8. Read what you have written. Ponder the images, feelings, perceptions, and ideas that came to you.

9. Feel the message in its wholeness. What has been said to you by the Spirit? What of God has been revealed?

10. Look again at what you have written. What you have recorded is about you. What aspects of yourself do you reveal?

11. In response to this total experience, write a prayer that expresses your deepest understanding of your being as you sit in the presence of God.

The Healings of Jesus

1. If you are dealing with a negative obsession—feelings or thoughts that persist in haunting you, read Mark 1:21–28 (a man with an evil spirit).

2. If you have a sense of guilt about a present or past behavior, a cancerous growth on your life, read Mark 1:40–45 (cleansing the leper).

3. If you feel helpless in a dimension of your life, unable to cope, read Mark 2:1–12 (healing a paralyzed man).

4. If you feel incompetent in performing a task, unable to function as effectively as you wish, read Mark 3:1–6 (the crippled hand).

5. If you have conflict with those who are near to you regarding your call and ministry, read Mark 3:31–35 (Jesus' mother and brothers).

6. If your life has lost its grounding and feels tossed and insecure, read Mark 4:35–41 (Jesus stills the storm).

7. If you feel your life divided, with conflicting desires pulling you in different directions, read Mark 5:1–20 (a man with evil spirits).

8. If you feel hopeless in your struggle and your energy is continually drained, read Mark 5:25–34 (the woman who touched Jesus' cloak).

9. If your life feels trapped in ritual and form without spirit and power, read Mark 7:1–8 (teachings of the ancestors).

10. If you have been ensnared by a set of legalisms, read Mark 7:14–23 (what makes a person clean/unclean).

11. If you feel blocked in your communication, read Mark 7:31–37 (healing of the deaf-mute).

12. If you have been unable to grasp the meaning of your life; if you have no sense of perspective for where you are in your life process, read Mark 8:22–26 (Jesus heals a blind man).

13. If you have been preoccupied with material success, read Mark 10:17–25 (the rich young ruler).

14. If you feel that nobody cares, no one seems to respond to your pain and need, read Mark 10:46–52 (Jesus heals Bartimaeus).

15. If you are facing an impossible situation in your life, one that you cannot endure in your own strength, read Mark 14:32–41 (prayer in Gethsemane).

16. If you have been betrayed by a friend, read Mark 14:43–50 (Judas' betrayal).

17. If you have felt forsaken, left alone to struggle with life, read Mark 14:66–72 (Peter's denial of Jesus).

18. If you have felt exposed, jeered at, made fun of, read Mark 15:16–20 (soldiers at the cross).

Exercise for Chapter 3
Listening to God in the Present Moment

This guide will help you reflect on the events of your day.

1. Sit quietly.

2. Pray for the illumination of the Spirit.

3. Name the events of your day.

4. Relive each event. Give thanks to God for it.

5. Confess the sin or brokenness that you discover.

6. What was the flow of the day, the movement forward?

7. What themes were repeated in your life?

8. Where does your life seem to be moving?

9. What new word did God seem to speak through the events?

10. Symbolize the day. Look at it as a whole. Contemplate the God who came to you in the clothing of those events.

Exercise for Chapter 4
Journey to the Desert

This chapter guided you into silence. After an attempt to be silent for a day, or even several days in retreat, reflect on the silence.

    1. What difficulties did I encounter?

    2. What did I find at my own center in the silence?

    3. What was the deepest impression I brought back from the silence?

    4. What benefits did I receive?

    5. Do I know someone with whom I could share the silence?

Exercise for Chapter 5
Spiritual Companionship
on the Journey

FINDING A SPIRITUAL COMPANION

The person I am considering as a spiritual guide is:

_____
(name)

I. Questions for me to ask

    1. Is this person spiritually mature?

    2. Does this person have a knowledge of scripture and the spiritual classics?

    3. Is this an accepting, affirming person?

    4. Will this person be honest with me?

    5. Can I trust what this person says to me?

    6. Will this person consider my request as a call from God?

II. Agreements to be negotiated with my spiritual companion

    1. A clear statement of our goals and expectations.

2. Whether the spiritual direction will be one way (for myself only) or mutual (for both of us).

3. A structure for the meetings.

4. A contract to meet for a stated period of time with the understanding that the relationship can be terminated.

Exercises for Chapter 6
Journey in the Kingdom Vision

1. For the next month spend time at the silent center, the point of convergence of all things. Bring to that center your world. Where do you fit in the larger scheme of things? What contribution can you make to the kingdom vision?

Over a period of weeks write the components of your vision of the kingdom of God. What is the new heaven and new earth that you envision for the future?

2. Read today's newspaper headlines. Picture the events they report. In what way do these events express or contradict the purpose of God in the world? Let your reflection on these events inform your prayers.

Appendix B

Journaling, an Important Tool for the Spiritual Journey

The spiritual journal finds a new importance in modern-day spirituality. Because of the discovery of journaling as an aid to spiritual growth, we will explore a number of possibilities for its use.

The spiritual journal records our spiritual pilgrimage; it becomes a place to meet God by listening to the data of our outward and inward life. Here we record the meaning of these data and integrate that significance into our life.

The journal provides a record of our perceptions of God's intervention in our life. This material describes the outer events of life, insights into scripture, the occurrences of a day, the data gathered through reading, research, and reflection. The journal records dreams, hopes, imaginings. These are the data with which we work.

A journal is also a place of meeting. The hard data of reality meet our dreams and goals. Fusing hard reality with the visions and values of our lives provides a setting for encountering the one who gives ultimate meaning.

The journal provides a place for decision and response. Writing our responses to the revelation of God through scripture, through inspiration, through image, through the events of life, makes the journal a place of accountability. It holds our response to God. In the future when we refer to the journal, the written commitment holds us accountable.

A journal facilitates integration. It is the matrix in which we connect the truth of today with the larger truth of our life. Not only does it connect with the larger flow of our personal life but with our primary community and, beyond that, with the purpose of God.

We enhance our growth as we use the journal to record the data of our lives brought to our consciousness by the work of the Spirit. The journal provides an arena in which truth is born, decisions are made, meaning is created, and accountability is established for the union of our lives with the purpose of God.

Uses of a Journal

The spiritual journal is not a diary. A diary contains occurrences, observations, and descriptions. The diary usually makes no effort to connect external events with an internal meaning and ultimately with the purpose of God. The spiritual journal, by contrast, seeks that end. While the journal collects external data, it does so primarily to discern their inner meaning.

A few suggestions may help. As you begin a journal, write regularly. Don't feel guilty if you miss a day. Experiment with the forms of journal writing as you feel comfortable. Work with one discipline until you have exhausted its use. For example, begin by recording your daily prayer experience. Ask what it meant or did not mean to you. Here are other specific ways in which you may use your journal.

1. Use the journal when you feel fragmented, when you lack a center. Begin writing by asking, "Where am I in my life?" Look at the events, the feelings, the use of time, your priorities, sin, activities, and significant persons or occurrences. As you write about these "happenings," get a "feel" for what is going on with you. This reflection helps to draw your life together.

2. Use the journal to project yourself into scripture. Record your meditations on scripture and the meanings that occur to you.

3. Use the journal to record your search for guidance. Ask, "What do I most want to do with my life?" List the possible answers. Then raise the question, "To what extent do these desires manifest or conflict with the Spirit of Jesus Christ?"

4. Use the journal to free yourself from rigid perceptions and commitments. Try to sort out your life and begin listening to God.

5. Use the journal to record your hunches and intuitions.

6. Use the journal to record your deepest conscious desires. Your deepest desires often portend the future. They signal the direction in which your life is moving.

7. Write your night dreams in your journal.

8. Use your journal to make confessions. On the pages of the journal you can say to God what you feel most deeply. Pour out your emotions. This enables you to externalize your sin, guilt, and conflict. Sometimes we do not trust another person enough to say all the things we need to say.

9. Finally, use the journal to make lists of persons for whom to pray. These are friends, family members, persons with whom you work, persons whom you meet in your daily life. If you write down their names and their specific needs, you will remember to pray for them.

Intercessory prayer is an important ministry of the church. Keeping lists of persons and situations about which we are praying will make us more disciplined in our prayers.

Values of Keeping a Journal

The journal offers a way to objectify our feelings and intuitions. It enables us to concretize and externalize them. Recording them in the journal gives a sense of relief, like having been pregnant with an idea or intuition and then being delivered of it. Writing detaches us from our dreams. In a way writing compares with telling another person: you make the idea or the sin or the confession external to yourself, and that enables you to be more objective in dealing with the data of your life.

Writing in a journal has an attracting, magnetic effect. In some ways writing draws out our depth more than talking to another person. Writing is like drawing water from a well. The rope has multiple buckets attached. Each word we write draws another and another. As we continue to pull, the line draws material out of us of which we were totally unaware.

We know more than we are aware of. We are aware of more than we can say. Writing has its own creative power that enables us to formulate knowledge we never consciously possessed.

Writing also clarifies our own thoughts. Thoughts that are vague and inexpressible become clearer when we write them down. For example, each time I ask the question, "Where am I in my life?" and write the answer, the data of my present experience become much sharper to me than before my writing.

Work in the journal invites dialogue. We may begin with the data of our lives, a dream, a vision, a passage of scripture. As we ask questions of that data, something within us responds. These dialogical experiences engage the material of our lives in a creative encounter that resolves conflict and integrates insights into the fabric of our lives.

The journal also helps us to discern the trends of our lives. When we read over a journal that contains two or three months' or two or three years' worth of writing, we can ask some critical questions:

1. What has had my attention for the last six months?
2. What has my energy been focused on?
3. What themes keep recurring in my life?
4. Where am I struggling, resisting the presence of God?
5. For what am I longing?

These kinds of questions presuppose that the concrete events of our lives reveal the work of the Spirit, enabling us to discern what the Spirit is doing and where the Spirit is leading us.

Getting Started with Journal Keeping

First, decide that you want to keep a journal. You may decide to keep a journal in conjunction with the various exercises in this text and in *To Will God's Will: Beginning the Journey*. Or you may decide to keep a journal permanently, a much more difficult decision to make and sustain.

Second, secure an appropriate notebook for your journal entries. My favorite is a bound record book, which may be obtained at any office supply store. Other teachers recommend a loose-leaf notebook. A friend of mine keeps his journal on a computer. You may choose a plain spiral notebook. Whatever you select, it should be easy to handle, simple to store, and private.

Date each entry in your journal—month, day, and year. When I began keeping a journal in my college days, I referenced entries only with a day and a month. Now I have no idea what year I wrote them. As time goes on, the years blend together, and it is impossible to remember when entries were made.

I like to write in longhand. Some persons prefer to type, but I favor a felt-tip pen and handwritten notes. For some reason I feel closer to handwritten notes than I do to typed ones. They seem to convey the feeling of my life more than the impersonal strokes of a typewriter key. Also, when I write by hand, my ideas take firmer shape as they flow onto the page.

As you begin a program of journal writing, you may wish to refer to Appendix B of *To Will God's Will* for Exercise 2, "The Chapters of Your Life." Doing this exercise will help you get an overview of the marker events of your life.

Let yourself be bold in experimenting with new ways to encounter God. The exercises in Appendix A of this book and in Appendix B of *To Will God's Will* provide ample suggestions for getting started.

Notes

Chapter 1: Meditation on the Journey

1. Urban T. Holmes III, *A History of Christian Spirituality* (New York: Seabury Press, 1981), pp. 3–4.

2. William Johnston, ed., *The Cloud of Unknowing and the Book of Privy Counseling* (New York: Doubleday & Co., Image Books, 1973), p. 48.

3. Thomas H. Green, S.J., *Opening to God* (Notre Dame, Ind.: Ave Maria Press, 1977).

4. Urban T. Holmes III, *Spirituality for Ministry* (San Francisco: Harper & Row, 1982), pp. 135–136.

5. F. C. Happold, *The Journey Inwards* (Atlanta: John Knox Press, 1968), p. 97.

6. Ibid.

7. Ibid.

8. Ibid., p. 101.

9. Quoted in Carlo Carretto, *Summoned by Love* (Maryknoll, N.Y.: Orbis Books, 1978), p. 19.

10. See exercise 2, "The Chapters of Your Life," in Appendix B of *To Will God's Will: Beginning the Journey* (Philadelphia: Westminster Press, 1987).

11. For this three-day silent retreat I went to the Monastery of the Holy Spirit in Conyers, Georgia. I structured the time with reading, reflection, quiet walks, writing in my journal, and composing letters to friends with whom I wan-

ted to share my prayers. Some time each day was set aside
to do "nothing." Someone has called this "wasting time
with God."

Chapter 2: Journey Into the Contemplation of God

1. Thomas A. Harris, M.D., *I'm OK—You're OK* (New
York: Harper & Row, 1969), pp. 4–12.
2. Holmes, *Spirituality for Ministry*, pp. 134–139.
3. Ira Progoff, *The Symbolic and the Real* (New York:
McGraw-Hill Book Co., 1973).

Chapter 3: Listening to God in the Present Moment

1. Frederick Buechner, *The Sacred Journey* (San Francisco: Harper & Row, 1982), p. 77.
2. Jean-Pierre de Caussade, *Abandonment to Divine
Providence* (Garden City, N.Y.: Doubleday & Co., Image
Books, 1975). The metaphors I have listed were gathered
from throughout the book.
3. Ibid., p. 28.

Chapter 4: Journey to the Desert

1. Holmes, *Spirituality for Ministry*, p. 62.
2. Henri J. M. Nouwen, *The Way of the Heart* (New York:
Seabury Press, 1981), p. 49.
3. Henri J. M. Nouwen, *The Genesee Diary: Report from
a Trappist Monastery* (Garden City, N.Y.: Doubleday & Co.,
1976), p. xii.
4. Nouwen, *The Way of the Heart*, p. 27.
5. Carlo Carretto, *Letters from the Desert* (Maryknoll,
N.Y.: Orbis Books, 1972), p. xvii.
6. Ibid., pp. 73–74.

Chapter 5: Spiritual Companionship on the Journey

1. Kenneth Leech, *Soul Friend: The Practice of Christian
Spirituality* (San Francisco: Harper & Row, 1980), p. 34.
2. Holmes, *Spirituality for Ministry*, p. 33.
3. Ibid., p. 36.

Chapter 6: Journey in the Kingdom Vision

1. Nouwen, *The Way of the Heart,* pp. 38–39.
2. Alan Paton, *Ah, But Your Land Is Beautiful* (New York: Charles Scribner's Sons, 1982), pp. 65–67.
3. Nouwen, *The Way of the Heart,* p. 35.
4. Carlo Carretto, *I Sought and I Found* (Maryknoll, N.Y.: Orbis Books, 1984), p. 131.

DATE DUE

Demco. Inc. 38-293